AMA

University of Nebraska Press: Lincoln and London

DIANE L. BARTHEL

From Pietist Sect

to American

Community

Publication of this book was
aided by a grant from The
Andrew W. Mellon Foundation.

The paper in this book meets
the guidelines for
permanence and durability
of the Committee on
Production Guidelines for
Book Longevity
of the Council on Library
Resources.

Library of Congress Cataloging
in Publication Data

Barthel, Diane L., 1949-
Amana : from Pietist
sect to American community.

Includes index.
1. Amana Society–History.
I. Title.
HX656.A4B37   1984
335'.97776   83-14624
ISBN 0-8032-1181-3

Contents

Illustrations

Preface

IN 1932 seven small German villages in southeastern Iowa—the Amana Colonies—faced a crucial decision, the most difficult of their long history as a religious sect. For 228 years their guiding doctrine had been an austere religious faith; for the past 88 years they had added to their original pietism a communal structure. Together they had shared work, goods, lives, and devotion, first in upstate New York, then, from 1856 on, in the fertile Iowa River valley where they had relocated seeking distance from the secular world. But that distance had proved illusory. For years the outside society had been giving vent to its curiosity, and strangers had been driving through the villages in their new Fords snapping photographs of the black-garbed communards. Worse, an internal defection was mounting among their own members as young men and women—the productive future of the community—stole away to Cedar Rapids, Iowa City, and Des Moines. There ruffled dresses and sharply cut suits, movies and automobiles tempted; there they could decide their own futures instead of dutifully accepting the work chosen for them by village elders.

This dual erosion had been occurring for decades. Changes in the outside society—growing industrialization, urbanization, and political centralization—were reflected inside the community. The village-based economy of small craft shops and farms, rational when the rest of the American economy was largely based on the small locality, became less rational with the rise of a truly national economy. A protocapitalism even developed within the communal structure, as the leaders reserved for themselves the privileged positions as teachers, doctors, and business managers, and as the members resorted to individualistic enterprises such as selling their craftwork or produce from their gardens to set up forbidden bank accounts. By the 1920s the community's woolen industry and its agricultural products could no longer compete with the more modern and efficient enterprises of the larger society. With the community ledger increasingly in the red, the Depression was the economic coup de grace, forcing community leaders to face the question long anticipated but long forestalled.

The choice put to the approximately one thousand remaining colonists was this: Would they all agree to a communal belt-tightening? Would they renounce worldly attractions to return to the strict values of their ancestors, thus safeguarding the communal structure they had devised, believing it to be sanctified by divine inspiration? Or would they compromise these values and this structure to integrate their lives into the mainstream of American society? Would they choose to embrace the secular world and the values of individualism, materialism, and capitalist profit their elders had so long and so passionately inveighed against?

Difficult as the situation was, the difficulty itself could have been interpreted by the community as a challenge to greater devotion. It might have inspired a reaffirmation of tradition and the superiority of community values. Choosing the outside world would mean, if not defeat, then at least recognition of a change so broad, of historic processes so overwhelming, that communal and religious commitment could not resist. The vote to forsake communalism thus truly was a "Great Change," as it became known throughout the community. Yet many residents experienced the decision as no real decision. As one woman who voted said afterward, "There was no real choice. There could be no going back."

With that, the former communards undertook a dramatic effort to catch up with the modern world. They held cocktail parties and formed 4-H clubs; they electrified their homes and nailed on aluminum siding. The corporation, inheritor of the control formerly exercised by the church, quickly closed down the craft shops and opened sandwich shops and gas stations, and a small business started by two young men to manufacture beer coolers soon grew into a major refrigeration company. The villages seemed indeed to have come a long way from their pietistic origins.

Yet, paradoxically, today there *is* a going back, though of a different sort. With some thirty thousand tourists a week crowding its narrow village streets, with campers and vans parked alongside ditches and blocking residents' driveways, with a growing list of tourist attractions and museums making it one of the "must see" stops of the Midwest, the Amana Colonies—now church society and capitalist corporation—have indeed joined American society. Amana microwave ovens and freezers are marketed worldwide; Amana woolens are sold in fabric stores across the nation; the farm department works what may rightly be considered the largest farm in Iowa; and the tourist business provides additional income for many residents. Secure in its present, Amana is now reevaluating its past. Residents, like tourists, are ready to search out the lessons in the morality play provided by their past utopian experience.

Amana thus figures importantly both in the history of communal experiments and in our contemporary social imagination. While journal and magazine articles on this community frequently appear, there exists to date no full and accessible history. My aim is to remedy this relative neglect the community has suffered, especially compared with the extensive literature on other communal societies such as Oneida or the Shaker communities.

Writing as a sociologist, I have integrated into the text theoretical concerns with sect formation and adaptation, charismatic leadership, and societal development. While many studies of communal and utopian societies have considered them as social laboratories in which human behavior can be studied apart from the contaminating influences of history and culture, I view Amana as responsive to and to some measure reflective of larger historical developments. In its move from communalism to capitalism, Amana, existing on the periphery of American society, has much to reveal about processes occurring at the society's center. In its transition we see reflected social trends that transformed communities throughout the United States, processes that created a new national culture, a new political structure, and a new national myth.

On a more symbolic level, the community's transition from religious sect to tourist attraction reflects a curious process whereby society and utopian groups create myths about each other. Each becomes involved in telling tales of the other's political structure and values based on the demands of its own politics and ideology. French Catholic poet Charles Péguy has written, "Everything begins as mystique and finishes as politics."[1] Yet, even more often, that which becomes politics reverts to myth. Under politics, we can include all that involves the use of power in making decisions on how a people should work and live, and how resources (from goods to power and prestige) should be distributed. Myth, in turn, may be considered as depoliticized speech, insofar as it takes the raw and unruly material of history, erases its contradictions and contingencies, and makes it all appear natural and thus immutable, undeniable. As Roland Barthes has said: "In passing from history to nature, myth acts economically; it abolishes the complexity of human acts, it gives them the simplicity of essences, it does away with all dialectics, with any going back beyond what is immediately visible, it organizes a world which is without contradictions because it is without depth, a world wide open and wallowing in the evident; it establishes a blissful clarity; things appear to mean something by themselves."[2]

Throughout the history of this one utopian group, myth and politics form a baroque pattern, with certain themes first sounded as myth later appearing as politics, and notes initially sounded as politics later reverberating as myth. As one such theme, the process of secularization took the initial religious myth, itself a product of its political times, and gave it form. It made of small study groups scattered throughout northern Europe in the early eighteenth century a political unit. It suggested the terms for early leadership struggles, for conflict with church and state au-

thorities throughout the eighteenth and early nineteenth centuries, and eventually formed the basis for the group's emigration
to the United States in 1844. Once on our shores, the group's inspired leadership made political decisions (specifically, their
adoption of communalism) that, though independent of the original religious myth, evolved into a second myth, becoming en-
dowed, as the definition suggests, with a supernatural justification. Thus when, in the early 1900s, both a new political order
and a new myth from the outside society were invading the community, the communal order under challenge was seen as result-
ing not from earlier political decisions but from the divine will of
the Lord. The new myth of modernity would gain the ascen-
dancy, however, and in time even Amana's religion would become
modernized.

The pull of modernity was hard to resist. Amana, like the rest
of the nation, would be attracted into participation in this new
national culture through such powerful lures as the motion
pictures, automobiles, Sears and Roebuck catalogs, fashions.
Amana people, like people elsewhere, learned how to be social
and how to consume. In time this pull of modern life forced a political transformation that in turn was interpreted in mythical
terms by the dominant society. The political and economic organization of the old Amana, initially serving to separate group
from society, was eventually destroyed by its inability to respond
to outside changes. Today, in contrast to earlier church-centered
control of political and economic matters, the corporation holds
most of the political power and the church is left with a more
purely symbolic role.

Yet now, though Amana has officially joined American society,
a whole new myth has developed out of its earlier structure. Now
that religious communalism has become history, it has developed
its own myth and spiritual attraction. In turn, a new political
structure is developing around this new myth, a structure reflected in the growing tourist presence and the current debate on
historic preservation of the Amanas. In the end we shall see that
we have finally come, in a sense, full circle. For, as anthropolo-
gists Victor and Edith Turner suggest, the tourist is not totally
unlike the religious pilgrim: each, in his or her own fashion, is

searching for and susceptible to a certain myth. "A tourist is half a pilgrim, if a pilgrim is half a tourist. Even when people bring themselves in anonymous crowds on beaches, they are seeking an almost sacred, often symbolic mode of communitas, generally unavailable to them in the structured life of the office, the shop floor, or the mine. Even when intellectuals, Thoreau-like, seek the wilderness in personal solitude, they are seeking the material multiplicity of nature, a life source."[3]

I myself came to Amana somewhat as a pilgrim. My mother had grown up there and left before the Change. As a girl, I visited the colonies several times and listened to stories of the old Amana. Coming back to conduct historical and field research in the summers of 1977–79, I found my entrée eased both by members of my extended family residing there and by the cooperation and assistance of individuals associated with the Museum of Amana History, the Amana Society, and the Amana Church Society. I undertook participant observation and also conducted both formal and informal interviews covering all aspects of community life and organization. Formal interviews were usually conducted at work, informal interviews at home. Out of respect for my informants and a desire to protect their anonymity, I have avoided identifying the sources of quotations in the text and have sometimes changed the identity of the village following a quotation. I also availed myself of unobtrusive methods such as noting the range, theme, and images of tourist products offered and significant changes in the physical landscape.

To the information so gathered I added study of historical material. This included extensive reading of secondary sources on early eighteenth and nineteenth century Germany, New York State and the Midwest, and comparative study of other communal societies. I added to examination of secondary sources on Amana my own reading of much of the primary material available, including the volumes of the *Inspirations-Historie*, the community *Bulletin*s published from 1932 to the present, and outside newspaper accounts. See my Bibliographical Essay for a full discussion of the sources consulted.

This book thus exists at the intersection of the personal and the theoretical. It is an interpretive history, one that uses Amana's historical course to raise questions that individuals and communities across the nation face as they come to terms with their individual and collective pasts.

Since this book has been seven years in the making, it has benefited from the comments and criticisms of friends and colleagues. I would like to thank my Harvard mentors George C. Homans and Seymour Martin Lipset. Various sections of the manuscript were read by David L. Bouchier, Maren Lockwood Carden, Lewis Coser, Rose Laub Coser, Dolores Hayden, Walter W. Powell, Michael Schudson, and Ann Swidler. During my year at the University of Essex, I benefited from the helpful comments of Leonore Davidoff and Paul Thompson and the assistance of the University of Essex library staff, notably Jane Long and Terry Tosetevin. In the final revision, Jonathan G. Andelson generously provided comments on the whole manuscript.

I owe a great debt to my mother, Lissette C. Barthel, for allowing me to open closed doors, and to Frieda Ehrmann, Selma Ehrmann, Rose Miller, and the late Carl Miller. I would also like to thank my extended Amana family and friends, though they are too numerous to list here. I should like to mention, however, the generous assistance of Henry Schiff and Madeline Roemig of the Museum of Amana History and Donald Shoup of the Amana Society. Photographs were provided by the Iowa Development Commission and the State Historical Society of Iowa. Translations from the *Inspirations-Histories* were done by my mother and by my father, Henry C. Barthel, a former teacher of German. Veronica Abjornson, Carole Roland, and Rosemarie Sciales typed the manuscript.

A special note of thanks goes to my sister, Carol Barthel, to whom this book is dedicated. I appreciate her careful reading, well-considered criticisms, and unflagging encouragement.

Pietist Faith, Communal Structure

PART I

The German Heritage

CHAPTER I

 In southern Germany in the year 1714, a small
group of men and women gathered to discuss matters of religious concern. This by itself was not surprising. Religious unrest was widespread throughout northern Europe, much of it
directed against a Lutheran church that had grown lax in its
own revolt against the abuses of Catholicism, joined hands with
state authorities, and increasingly engaged in scholastic debate
rather than answering the needs of the simple people who tried
to gain salvation through following its tenets. This small group,
which included a few renegade Lutheran ministers, objected to
this establishment orientation and looked instead to its own vision of early Christianity. The members were pietists, so called
because they wished to live in simple piety—to carry worship
into their lives, sharing the religious philosophy of the Mennonites and Hutterites and numerous smaller sects.[1] Where
they differed is in their distinctive history and peculiar fate.

Little did this small group know that in its religious search it
was laying the basis for a society—the Society of True Inspiration—that would suffer abrupt transformations but would endure to the present day. One hundred years after its founding it
would be at the nadir of its existence, restricted to a few small
cells of believers scattered across northern Europe. Fifty years
later, in 1864, it would be at its zenith, a communal sect in distant Iowa, prospering and providing a secure life for approxi-

mately fifteen hundred members. In 1914, though still seeming solid and secure, its calm exterior would belie inroads by the outside society that would lead to dramatic change, so that in 1974 —two hundred and fifty years after that first group met to discuss the need to effect God's will on earth—the Society would be prospering as a capitalist corporation.

These transformations happened neither by accident nor by caprice. They were in each case a reasoned response to winds of change that swept sect and society, altering both, leaving neither believer nor nonbeliever untouched.

EARLY BEGINNINGS

The first wind to set the Society off on its historic course was pietism, a religious movement that arose in Europe after the Thirty Years War (1618–48).[2] Several tendencies had been developing within the Lutheran church establishment, to which many ministers and laypeople objected in the belief that they were contrary to the true spirit of Protestantism. As its early revolt against the Catholic church became transformed into strong command over religious life and institutions, the Lutheran church appeared less concerned with winning converts and saving souls and more interested in debating increasingly abstruse points of doctrine. Moreover, the higher church leadership to some extent took responsibility for the common people's religious well-being away from their pastors and placed it in the hands of the local princes. Not only did the local aristocracy appoint ministers to their parishes, they also could periodically examine their subjects regarding their religious state.[3] Then also, the church was criticized for becoming worldly and hierarchical: churches had separate theaterlike boxes for the aristocracy, and ministers addressed the common people with the familiar "*Du*" but used the more respectful "*Sie*" for the aristocracy.[4] Thus, whereas earlier reform movements had generally originated with theologians, the pietism of the period after 1650 derived most of its support from the local ministers and from craftspeople, domestic servants, and peasants.[5]

After 1650 literacy increased rapidly among these groups,

and many common people became familiar with pietist religious tracts.[6] Philipp Spener (1635–1705) and August Herman Francke (1663–1727), usually considered the founders of pietism, criticized orthodox Lutheran theology for what Spener termed its neglect of the "personal experience of justification . . . the actual experience of the terrors of conscience by the individual Christian."[7] But other texts were also popular, including many with a decidedly mystical edge. Johann Arndt's *True Christendom* was well known and often reprinted up to the early nineteenth century, as were tracts relating the mystical doctrines of Jakob Boehme of Gorlitz, a shoemaker/philosopher.[8]

This movement received a strong boost after the War of the Spanish Succession in 1712–13, when Frederick William I of Prussia became interested in its doctrines and even established the University of Württemberg as a center for pietist study. It is in this historical setting that the small group that was to become the Society of True Inspiration began meeting to discuss pietist ideas and tracts. Three brothers—A. F. Pott (who had studied at Halle, then a leading center of pietist thought), J. T. Pott, and J. H. Pott—had been holding meetings in the years 1708 to 1712. They were joined in time by others, including Johanna Melchior, daughter of a butcher, her brother-in-law Gottfried Newmann, and Eva Catherine Wagner, described as a married woman who lived "auf der Ronneburg"—on an estate that would become a leading Inspirationist center. This small group traveled and preached about the provinces of Ysenburg and Wittgenstein in southern Germany. In the fall of 1714 they arrived at Himbach, where they met two others of strong pietist orientation—Johann Frederick Rock and Eberhard Ludwig Gruber, both originally from Württemberg. Rock, son of a minister, was a harnessmaker, and Gruber had studied for the ministry. Rock had already been expelled from Stuttgart for holding meetings the town fathers deemed in opposition to the authority of the established church. The records list 6 November 1714 as the historic day when representatives of the first group met with Rock and Gruber. On this occasion, according to the community historian, Gruber was inspired "to do what was demanded of him; to erect a Brotherly Community of Prayer." In the course of their discussions, these pietists adopted many of the ideas of Spener and Boehme, but they added a more peculiar, clearly mystical belief.[9]

Central to the emergent Inspirationist dogma was the idea that now, as in the days of the prophets, God would speak directly to humankind through certain chosen individuals who would be called "*Werkzeuge*," or instruments. These instruments would give expression to God's word through writing or, more often, through speech. Under inspiration the *Werkzeug* would usually shake, seem to lose control, then deliver the *Bezeughungen*, or testimonies. Clearly, the presence of a *Werkzeug* supposedly speaking the word of God might dampen the uninspired individual's belief in his or her own ability to interpret the Bible. Thus, in a curious fashion, the Inspirationists might be seen as undoing some of the work of the Reformation. If the paradox of the Reformation was that authoritarian leaders like Calvin and Luther provided a path for greater individual freedom of interpretation, in this delicate balance between authority and freedom the Inspirationists added weight to the side of authority. Also, since conversion to pietism usually occurred through personal contact, many pietist sects had at their center some charismatic figure. For the *Werkzeuge*, inspiration became a pathway to charismatic authority and appeal—and of course to power.[10]

Rock himself was quickly declared a *Werkzeug*, as later were other members, but he alone was able to maintain his power for an extended period.[11] Gruber never gained inspiration, but he did provide the nascent community with specific guidelines for religious thought and behavior known as the Twenty-one Rules for the Examination of Daily Life. In these rules would-be followers were told, for example, "to obey without reasoning, God, and through God, our superiors." They were "to study quiet, or serenity, within and without." Selflessness was stressed, as was sobriety of thought and manner. The attitude toward fellow members was to "Live in love and pity toward your neighbor." The correct attitude toward outsiders was simply to "Have no intercourse with worldly minded men; never seek their society: speak little with them, and never without need; and then not without fear and trembling." Abstinence and control were to be practiced regarding food and drink—"Dinners, weddings, feasts avoid en-

tirely; at the best there is sin"—and also in other matters—"Fly
from the society of women as much as possible, as a very highly
dangerous magnet and magical fire." This last injunction, which
reflects the negative attitude toward women that runs as an un-
dercurrent through Christianity, was certainly never applied
with any thoroughness; though discouraged, marriage was accepted as a necessary institution. In their admixture of pietism
and Lutheranism, Inspirationists also followed a version of the
Apostles' Creed, the Twenty-four Rules for True Godliness, the
Ten Commandments, and the Lord's Prayer.[12]

During the early 1700s other pietist groups were also active.
One group of Moravian brethren, excited by reports of William
Penn's vision and plans for Pennsylvania, followed him and became the basis for the widely known Amish settlements.[13] Others
gathered under the leadership of Count Zinzendorf, who in 1722
founded the brethren's community in Herrnhut, Saxony, whose
members later became known as the Herrnhutters. They followed a more generous and accepting line than did the Inspirationists, believing that people were essentially good and that
"through sensual and spiritual contemplation of Christ divine
strength would fill the human soul."[14] Zinzendorf's settlements,
which accepted anyone who professed to worship Christ, soon
became centers of pietism, governed by elders and linked by a
loose synodal structure. In the 1730s Rock visited Zinzendorf's
community, and Zinzendorf returned the compliment by visiting
the Inspirationists. During these years there was much talk of a
possible merger, but in the end neither leader was willing to sacrifice leadership or theological distinction. Zinzendorf appears to
have been particularly annoyed by Rock's gift of inspiration,
which on one occasion was directed against the count himself.
On another occasion Zinzendorf said he would talk to Rock if
Rock would agree to restrain his inspiration. The latter predictably responded that inspiration "is nothing with which to trifle or
compromise. It is God's and so it shall remain." Thus, instead of
joining together the Herrnhutters and Inspirationists remained
in competition for converts and sources of support in the areas
around the Ronneburg estate.[15]

Other problems faced the Inspirationists as the 1740s wore on.

Gruber had died in 1728; Rock grew increasingly feeble in the late forties and died in 1749. In addition, after the 1740s pietist ideas increasingly lost official favor as the Enlightenment reached deeper into Germany and Europe.[16] This ideological change, compounded by the political turmoil throughout Europe in the latter half of the eighteenth century and early nineteenth century, placed the Inspirationists on the defensive.[17] They retreated to a few estates scattered through northern France, Switzerland, and Germany and watched as one after another of the old members and elders died. Though they lamented their decline, they voiced little hope for the future.

REVIVAL

By the early 1800s, however, new forces encouraged the sect's revival. Germany at this time was still a collection of large estates and provinces. Although some had been exposed to the new French democratic ideals, others like Prussia were still under the control of the powerful landed aristocracy. With the end of the Napoleonic wars in 1815, the aristocracy swung back toward social and political conservatism. But they were countering powerful social trends that eventually resulted in the revolution of 1848. In the early 1800s, these social trends were beginning to make themselves felt, not just by aristocrats but by the commoners: peasants, domestic servants, craftspeople.

The German peasants were freed from serfdom by a series of land reforms that started in 1807 and lasted through the early 1820s. But the main question was, Freed for what? The edicts and reforms broke the traditional ties of responsibility between nobleman and peasant, yet they did little to establish new economic structures that would allow the peasants to earn a living. "After centuries of bondage," writes Theodore Hamerow describing the peasant's plight, "he was left to shift for himself in a world of bankers, industrialists, and landlords."[18] Individual peasants had few resources and little land, since already small plots were further divided among the children. Many also still carried the burden of fixed rents and services due to noblemen turned landlords.[19]

The peasants were not alone in their plight. Domestic servants had often been considered members of the household, on a level with the master's children, with status determined by age and length of service. By the early 1800s, however, this family relationship was being replaced by that of employer/employee, usually with a loss of status for the servant.[20]

But perhaps the greatest changes affected craftspeople. Artisans—the shoemakers, watchmakers, coopers, and cabinetmakers, the tailors and the weavers—had been strictly organized by powerful guilds that controlled admittance, standards, pricing, and production.[21] This organization of work was an integral part of village and town structure, a total way of life. As Hamerow describes it:

> The handicraft system had made possible an organization of manufacture suitable to a static communal order. It was designed to meet the needs of a stable population, to maintain an unchanging standard of living, to supply a market local in scope. . . . The advantages inherent in mechanical efficiency and competitive individualism were renounced for the sake of security and order.[22]

Though it was static only by comparison with later periods, this is the way of life that craftspeople and peasants alike found threatened in early-nineteenth-century Germany. It was this quasi-communal, village-centered order that the Inspirationists would in time carry with them to the United States.[23] This older form of economic organization increasingly came under attack by that major cutting edge of industrialization, the factory system. Among the first major trades affected was weaving, and the Inspirationists attracted a number of disaffected weavers—enough, in fact, to establish their own mill. When this competition from factories in England and in Germany was added to the progressive reduction of guild control in the German states, it is no wonder many an artisan experienced 1820–48 as "years of crisis, years when government, technology, and fate all seemed to conspire to encompass his ruin."[24]

All these trends were aggravated by the tremendous growth in population.[25] Between 1815 and 1845 the population of Germany rose from 25,000,000 to 34,500,000, a growth of 38 percent, causing serious overpopulation in the South and West.[26] This sudden expansion exacerbated other social processes and tensions, creating great land hunger, providing workers for the new factory system, further undermining the artisan trades, and leading to mass emigration.[27] Under this economic deprivation, many turned to the ideas of socialism and found their answer in revolution. Others, however, looked to religion—some back to pietism.

Pietism was still popular among the common folk, pietists being called "*die Stillen im Land*"—the quiet people in the countryside. During this period some believers joined their pietism to Lutheran orthodoxy, stressing the need to marry altar to throne, Christian faith to the conservative belief in the divine right of princes. Others, however, continued in their original separatism, the sect-creating tradition in which the Inspirationists clearly participated.[28]

All these nascent social and religious forces made themselves felt as early as 1816–17, years that have been called "the last great subsistence crisis."[29] Artisans and industry were reeling under the loss of the war economy and under increased competition from English factories. Agriculture, already debilitated by wartime pillaging, was dealt another blow by adverse weather. In 1816 "summer never came." Poverty and famine were widespread.[30]

In this historical setting one Michael Krausert, as a journeyman tailor with no great economic expectations, reported a mystical experience to Inspirationist elders at the barely surviving settlement at Bischweiler, in Alsace. Not receiving guidance on the matter from skeptical superiors, two local elders at Bischweiler took it upon themselves to declare Krausert truly inspired. He then began to travel, like Rock and Gruber before him, preaching pietist doctrine and attracting followers.[31]

This same year, 1817, a number of young men at the Ronneburg estate in Hesse had organized with the aim of rekindling the faith. Two of their number, in opposition to elders content with the status quo, traveled to hear Krausert and were greatly impressed by him. One of these, Christian Metz, was to become the key figure in the group's history. Metz, the twenty-two-year-old son of an old Inspirationist, was short and broad-shouldered, with brown eyes and an oval face. His initial meeting with Krausert and his uncertainty about Krausert's inspiration appear to have led to a conversion experience. Metz underwent what his biographer Duval describes as a period of spiritual battle: he was overcome by weeping, then experienced repentance and a great inner peace.[32] He decided to join Krausert in his work.

Another who accepted Krausert's inspiration in these early years of revival was Barbara Heinemann, "a poor and illiterate servant maid" from Alsace. At the age of eight she had been sent out to work in a factory spinning wool. In 1813, in the financial crisis after the Napoleonic wars, the factory closed and Heinemann went to work as a servant. Perkins and Wick describe the ensuing change in the young woman's personality:

While she worked in the factory she had been of a lively disposition; now a peculiar state of mind bordering on melancholy suddenly clouded her lively temperament. She frequently attended church, for, if she engaged constantly in prayer, she thought this gloom might pass away. . . . One woman said she acted like the Pietists, of which people Barbara had never heard.[33]

Heinemann then went in search of a pietist community at Sulz and was there at the time of a visit by Krausert. He took an interest in her, explained the source of her depression, and predicted that she would become inspired, which she did on Christmas Day 1818, at the age of twenty-three.[34] Heinemann in turn prophesied that Metz would become inspired, and in a few months he did become the third of the new instruments of God.

A leadership struggle ensued, reflecting the instability of charismatic authority.[35] Krausert, after conflicts with Metz and Heinemann, finally had to admit that he might no longer be inspired, thus effectively resigning his leadership. Heinemann too was to suffer. In 1823 she married George Landmann, a teacher, and subsequently lost her own gift for inspiration, which she did not recover for twenty-six years.[36] During the crucial period of the community's development, Metz was left as the one *Werkzeug* and leader.

In the 1820s and 1830s Metz alternated periods of travel and recruitment with periods of consolidation. The Inspirationists leased several castles and adjoining estates, the center of their activity being the province of Hesse-Darmstadt, northeast of Frankfurt. In the 1830s Switzerland began requiring oaths of allegiance to the government. The Swiss Inspirationists refused to take these oaths, so they moved to the Inspirationist center and leased three more estates to house them and other members from Württemberg and Alsace.[37]

On these estates the Inspirationists seem to have by necessity accepted a degree of informal communalism, though the few accounts differ in exactly how much was present at this period in the community's history. Perkins and Wick write that:

> The members lived for the most part together in the castle or adjoining buildings, and in a large room in the castle meetings were held, and the children were taught; they worked the land together, sold the products and divided the proceeds equally. At first they did not eat at the same table, but when they saw that it would be cheaper to eat together this plan was adopted.
>
> Here we have the first beginnings of the communistic life, which the Society afterwards adopted. It arose unconsciously, from small beginnings, with no thought of what results would flow from it.[38]

Duval, however, minimizes this communalism by writing, "It is true that there had been a kind of communal life in Germany, but each member plied his own trade. Some remained poor, while others became financially independent, or even wealthy; thus the *Gemeinde* in Germany was essentially capitalistic."[39]

Although Metz was assisted throughout this period by his elders and their counsel, it was his gift of inspiration that was continually used to reaffirm his leadership and the legitimacy of the group faith and structure. The text of the inspirations reflects the general style of eighteenth-century writings, with considerable use of Old Testament phraseology. One testimony, recorded in 1833, finds Metz expressing the Lord's displeasure with those who claimed to possess mystical powers outside the legitimated structure. Particularly interesting is his use of a mystical vocabulary to condemn mysticism:

> Hear Ye: This is the will of God and shall remain for the members of this church. I have brought you along this way and guided you through the path of secret wisdom wherein you cannot err concerning the doors of

entrance; where the soul, the believing and faithful soul, cannot err because the way of life is altogether too clear. . . .

But those who would follow a different light, who would follow a mystic or magic light—to such the true word is not sufficient, and they have no understanding of the secret wisdom of God. They have the wrong key to the door. . . .

Do not accept the false keys to the secret and mystic and magic influences. . . . The soul has to be humble, simple, and small; it has to follow the path of obedience to satisfy its friend the father and bridegroom. This is the ground upon which I have founded and built this church, through the apostles and true teachers. My prophetic spirit is in their midst to discover and reveal all secret evil and the false prophecies that lead you astray. . . .

Blessed is the soul that understands and obeys and is loyal to it unto life's end.[40]

Thus this particular myth—the pietist belief in the realization of God's will through obedience and humility—provided the framework for the political structure and the basis for its legitimation. In this process political structures also evolved their own myths, which then served as further legitimation and means of control. The *Werkzeug* concept proved a most effective means of legitimating authority. Not just anyone could claim the gift of inspiration: in the early years Gruber's son was charged with the task of detecting false instruments.[41] Krausert himself, when he was forced to abandon the political struggle, did so through admitting he might no longer be inspired.

Like their forebears a century earlier, the nineteenth-century Inspirationists had to contend with religious competition from the outside. Charles Nordhoff, writing in 1875, describes the 1822 visit of a Quaker minister from London to the Inspirationists' settlement. He persuaded them to hold a religious meeting and to read the fourteenth chapter of the Gospel of John, predicting that he would then be inspired to speak to them. But at the actual meeting Barbara Heinemann was moved to speak before him. "At this Allen [the Quaker] became impatient and left the meeting," writes Nordhoff, telling the Inspirationists that Quaker inspiration was as true as their own, except that Quakers did not write it down. Whereupon the Inspirationists replied that the Quakers didn't have to, "for it was evident that the Quakers had not the real inspiration, nor the proper and consecrated 'instruments' to declare the will of the Lord." Nordhoff concludes by remarking that that Quaker "went away on his journey home, apparently not much edified."[42]

Given the key role of inspiration, one might ask why there was not a constant struggle for control, with large numbers of people claiming this special ability instead of merely a handful. The answer probably lies in the fact that there was another less difficult avenue to power within the community, one in which justification lay in temporal rather than spiritual abilities. For a man could also assume power through being nominated an elder. Metz was an effective leader in part because he rewarded his friends and wealthy recruits with elderships, thus ensuring their cooperation and circumventing their competition for authority. The structure of *Werkzeug* and elders also ensured that the potentially charismatic quality of inspired leadership would be fully grounded in a mini-bureaucracy that would temper the tie between leader and followers.

The religious myth also set the terms for the political struggle with the secular world. During this period following 1815 Germany was under the conservative tide, yet pockets of political liberalism were allowed to remain, as in the provinces of Hesse. But this tolerance was wearing thin, and since the Inspirationists' theology opposed the established Lutheran church, closely linked to state power, their politics were by definition in opposition to the state authorities. Throughout their period in Germany—from 1714 to 1844—the Inspirationists faced periodic outbreaks of persecution. They had gathered together in Hesse-Darmstadt largely because it was one of the most liberal provinces. In the face of rising conservatism and nationalism, even this tolerance faded, and the community again faced persecution by mobs and conflict with the state over its members' refusal to do military service or send their children to state schools, then in the hands of the Lutheran church. The community moved on to other estates within Hesse as necessary, ever attracting more followers— partly because, despite opposition and the high taxes it had to pay, the group was prospering. By 1840 it is estimated there were some 350 to 400 members living on the estates[43] and another 600 scattered throughout Germany, Alsace, and Switzerland. In 1840–41, however, a severe drought cut into this prosperity, a precursor of ever more severe droughts to follow throughout the 1840s. In 1842 Metz received word that the authorities would refuse to grant citizenship to foreigners residing on the estates.[44]

That notice appears to have been the final straw. As early as 1826 there had been hints of an eventual emigration to America in Metz's testimony, but it was on the very day he heard of this refusal of citizenship that Metz, under inspiration, told the community: "Your goal and your way shall lead toward the west to the land which is still open to you and your faith. I am with you and shall lead you over the sea. Hold Me, call upon Me through your prayers when the storm of temptation arises. . . . Four may then prepare themselves."[45]

Four men were chosen and prepared themselves for the arduous journey. The small party left the Armenburg estate in Hesse at 10:00 P.M. on 5 September 1842 after a solemn communion service. Their trip by mail coach to the coast was uneventful if uncomfortable. Arriving in Bremen on 10 September, they waited another six days, then traveled by steamer down the Weser to Bremerhaven, where they boarded the vessel *New York* for America.[46]

In their emigration, the Inspirationists formed part of what would swell to a massive wave of emigration, not just from Germany but from Ireland and Scandinavia as well. In Germany those who left were often not those who suffered the greatest absolute deprivation, but those who suffered the greatest relative deprivation—neither the poorest nor the richest.[47] The decision of such emigrants was based not so much on seeking out a radically new future as on protecting their past way of life. As Mack Walker writes:

The *Auswanderer* went to America less to build something new than to regain and conserve something old, which they remembered or thought they did . . . which the new Europe seemed determined to destroy. . . . They wanted to *escape* rootlessness . . . or rather, they felt their roots being torn up, and sought a place to sink them again, for they could not contemplate living another way. . . . They were conservatives, who acted radically in order to preserve, and who journeyed to another world to keep their homes.[48]

The decision to emigrate was undoubtedly most agonizing. Had the Inspirationists remained in Germany, they would have faced further drought, depression, and political turmoil. The very year of their leaving saw a revolt of weavers in Silesia that was cruelly suppressed, later to be memorialized in Gerhard Hauptmann's play *Die Weber*.[49] The Inspirationists' choice was to strike out for the new land, like so many of their compatriots. But in one regard they differed radically from these other German craftspeople and peasants, for once in this country they worked out an ingenious solution for their collective survival: these pietists became communards.

Ebenezer, New York

CHAPTER 2

T̲HE Inspirationists were far from the first to attempt communal life on American soil. By 1843, the year of their
arrival, communal societies were already a marked if irregular
feature of the American landscape. The Shakers, the most successful in terms of numbers, had communities extending from
Maine out to Ohio and down to Kentucky. These celibate worker/
worshipers had just gained new impetus and inspiration through
a revival in the 1830s, born of the supposed reappearance in a
vision of their founder, Mother Ann Lee. While the Shakers were
predominantly American recruits, Germans were often the raw
material of utopian communities. In 1804 George Rapp had led
his pietists away from the established church at Württemberg to
found the settlement at Harmony, Pennsylvania, which in 1815
moved to New Harmony, Indiana, then came back to Economy,
Pennsylvania, ten years later. A number of "Rappites," lured
away from Economy by an imposter named Count de Leon, later
formed the nucleus for two other communal societies at Bethel,
Missouri, and Aurora, Oregon. In 1817 yet another group of Germans from the provinces of Bavaria, Württemberg, and Baden
had arrived and emigrated to Zoar, Ohio, where they built their
large communal houses, mills, and factories.[1]

The Inspirationists knew of the group at Zoar and had communicated with them several times. Some members also were familiar with the ideas of Etienne Cabet, presented in his now-famous

volume *Voyage en Icarie*, published in 1841.[2] This volume provided the blueprint for groups who called themselves Icarians, which included one much-beleaguered group that would try, unsuccessfully, to establish a communal settlement in Texas and later again face difficulties in maintaining their community in western Iowa.

These Icarians, as one scholar of such communities remarked, "had only theory as an integrative force."[3] High ideals, often socialist, inspired many a utopian attempt between 1800 and 1850. Yet often ideals alone were insufficient to hold communities together. Robert Owen, a high-minded British industrialist/reformer who saw no need for conflict between enlightened owners and their workers, bought the site at New Harmony from the Rappites to establish a community where the principle of self-interest would be replaced by that of communal interest. Another major utopian thinker, Charles Fourier, dreamed of a society where social institutions would be founded on attraction rather than coercion; his ideas gained widespread popularity and led to the formation of more than forty utopian communities in the 1840s.

Besides communities based like these on ideals imported from Europe, there were others that developed more directly out of American social and religious thought, though with considerable cross-fertilization. John Humphrey Noyes studied theology at Yale, but his unconventional ideas made him break with the theological establishment and led in 1838 to his setting up a small community of family and friends in Putney, Vermont. Some eight years later he had persuaded the members to establish a controversial form of group marriage—certainly controversial among the neighboring Vermont farmers, who forced Noyes's group out of Vermont and westward to Oneida, in New York State, where they prospered into the 1870s. Three years before the Inspirationists' arrival, utopian communities were also to be found at Hopedale, Massachusetts, and, as memorialized in Nathaniel Hawthorne's *The Blithedale Romance*, at Brook Farm. In 1843 writer and thinker Bronson Alcott founded his Fruitlands at Harvard, Massachusetts. And in 1844 in Carthage, Illinois, the site to which the Mormons had fled from persecutions in New

York State, Joseph Smith, the Mormon prophet, announced his candidacy for president of the United States. In the same year, Joseph Smith was murdered.[4]

Thus the land was rich with communal experiments in the year of the Inspirationists' immigration, some faring well, others already in decline. Of all these groups the Inspirationists most closely resembled the Zoarites and the Rappites, who came from the same cultural background and were propelled by a similar religious impetus. Yet the fate of each group effort depended not just on its own social structure and ideology, but also on where and when the group settled—in other words, on the society immediately outside the commune's boundaries.

WESTERN NEW YORK

The area of central and western New York into which the Inspirationists were moving was no longer frontier. It had already experienced its period of tremendous land speculation, with major developers buying up huge tracts of land. People had flocked into the state from New England, and leading towns had quickly taken shape: Rochester, Albany, Syracuse, Buffalo. The immigrants had brought with them their religious concerns, which in this new setting erupted into near-frenzy. From approximately 1825 to 1850, middle New York State experienced what is now termed the Second Great Awakening, as religious revivalists like the powerful Charles Finney stressed their anti-intellectual, here-and-now brand of enthusiastic evangelism, peculiarly consonant with both the social background of the converts and the industrial needs of the region. So great was the revival and sect activity that the region earned the title "the burned-over district."[5]

By the time of the Inspirationist arrival, however, religious enthusiasm was at a simmer rather than a boil, with people apparently more concerned with getting down to business. Buffalo, only a half-day ride by cart from what would be the Inspirationist settlement at Ebenezer, was enjoying a success largely due to its having been chosen as western terminus of the Erie Canal, completed in 1825. That year Buffalo's population was a mere 5,141.

By 1855 it had soared to 74,214,[6] including a German colony of almost 30,000. These Germans, though predominantly Evangelical Lutherans, also included both ultraorthodox Lutherans and pietists. In this city, and especially within this population, the ideas of Owen and Fourier were given a serious hearing: several Fourierist phalanxes were attempted, and several German cooperative shops were opened. Later, in the 1850s, Marxian socialism would establish a beachhead among this same population.

The Inspirationists themselves, at the time of their arrival, were more interested in establishing their own communities than in debating ideas that seemed confined to the clouds. They were less interested in socialist discussion of what might be than in protecting, through their communal strategies, their image of what was: the village-based structure of an already-fading Germany. Facing them now was not just the physical construction of community, but also its social construction. How would they live, work, and govern themselves? What relations would they form with their new neighbors, these new Americans?

BUILDING COMMUNITY

After the word of inspiration, in September 1842 four men had formed a party to investigate land possibilities in the United States. The small group comprised George Weber, a physician; William Noe, who was considered "informed on business matters"; Gottlieb Ackermann, who practiced the old profession of *Bader*, a barber/surgeon who bled people with leeches; and Metz, who was then forty-seven years old. They departed from the community on 5 September 1842, and on 20 September they took ship for their thirty-seven-day crossing. Arriving in New York harbor on 26 October, they found a land agent who had been recommended by the ship's captain. Metz questioned the agent about land in Ohio, but he replied that the state was already fairly well settled. Then Wisconsin was mentioned, but the agent had heard of some settlers who had not fared well. Then the agent suggested New York State—Chautauqua County to be exact— where some land had recently come on the market. So the small party left New York City, traveling by steamer up to Albany, then across the state to Buffalo on an Erie Canal barge. At Buffalo they lodged at a hotel called the Mansion House, with which one Philip Dorscheimer was associated. Upon learning that the Inspirationists were there to look at land, he and two other leading German citizens (a local physician and the publisher of the local German newspaper) suggested they look at the Seneca Indian Reservation, whose lands had recently been opened for white settlement.[7]

The small party traveled the four miles out along the Aurora Buffalo Road to view the land. The reservation was still heavily wooded, despite its Indian villages, a church and mission, and land already under cultivation. As described poetically by a later historian, it may have seemed to their eyes "a primeval forest standing upon pleasantly rolling ground, a dim and solemn place drained by small watercourses which flowed through leafy hollows into Buffalo Creek."[8]

Metz was taken with the site, so the land company representatives were approached. Although the group viewed other sites, their thoughts returned to Buffalo Creek. They made a second trip, this time through a snowy landscape. "The prospect was very pleasing, their love for the Reservation had taken deep root and they concluded to draw up a tentative sale contract for 10,000 acres at $10.50 an acre."[9] Unfortunately, a series of misunderstandings and deceptions then commenced that eventually led to an initial purchase of only five thousand acres and that triggered a long dispute with the Indians over title to the land.[10]

The title dispute did not, however, stop the Inspirationists from settling and building on the land. In 1843 the first 350 Inspirationists immigrated, and by 1845 there were more than eight hundred members.[11] An early letter sent back by one of the first had warned the others not to expect to go "walking under the walnut trees." It warned, "There is much work to be done," no time for dreams of a leisured existence. The first village laid out was called Mittel Ebenezer (Middle Ebenezer), followed by Ober (Upper), Nieder (Lower), and Neue (New) Ebenezer. Two other small settlements were founded across the Canadian border. The German model is evident in the relative self-sufficiency of the villages, each containing its own craft shops, kitchens, bakery, meat market, school, and store. A sawmill was constructed at Ober, and the woolen mill, soap works, and vinegar mill were all at Mittel.[12] Flat board fences protected village property and farmland.

More difficult than erecting the physical structure of community was devising community organization. The move to the United States clearly presented the group with a rare opportunity, the chance to draw lessons from their experience on the German estates and to experiment in the new American setting. Indeed, of all the immigrants arriving during this period, why were the Inspirationists—stolid artisans, craftspeople, merchants—among the few to adopt the communal mode? The answer is far from obvious, but it may be related to their having lived together on the German estates. There, since the Society paid rents to its landlords in total, they had instituted a system where everyone worked in shops and farms held in common and all were paid for their services. They certainly were familiar with the practices of the old German craft guilds, which required cooperation among members. Several knew of Etienne Cabet's 1841 *Voyage en Icarie*, and Metz himself was aware of the settlement at Zoar, which he had visited while the question of the Ebenezer land title was still unsettled.[13] Nordhoff, a writer who later visited the community in Iowa, suggested that the need for capital to set up the woolen mill and to underwrite the poorer members encouraged a pooling of resources, and Bertha Shambaugh, writing in 1910, corroborated this by suggesting that early plans for private ownership of real estate were scuttled when it was realized that members were unequal in both talents and finances. Certainly for the poorer peasants among the transplanted Inspirationists communal support would prove preferable to the life they might anticipate on their own; for the wealthier who had contributed funds, the move to communalism could be seen as strengthening their leadership by increasing the social control they exercised. Three of the wealthiest members did propose that a permanent constitution be adopted supporting the communal structure.[14]

For all members, communalism was one workable means of organization and order in what must have been a difficult new situation. Significantly, the communal structure demonstrated certain elective affinities with the Inspirationist brand of pietism, especially its emphasis on the values of simplicity and self-surrender. In any case, the agreement of all members on this principle should not be exaggerated: as late as the 1850s dissension existed on the subject. In 1854 Metz finally felt it necessary to express through inspiration the Lord's condemnation of those who rejected the communal principle:

As truly as I live says the Lord, it is at no time my will to dissolve the ties of the community in such manner or to suffer its dissolution, neither through artful devices or skill or diplomacy nor cunning or power of men. . . . And there shall come eternal disgrace, shame, and disfavor upon those who cause it, their children shall suffer want and be without blessing in time and eternity. Their material possessions shall melt away and the divine treasures they have disavowed; therefore, the Lord is against them.[15]

This testimony apparently silenced the last holdouts, as we hear little more on the subject. The actual constitution adopted in 1846 differed significantly from the provisional one only in substituting yearly allotments for wages and through the stipulation that no interest would be paid in the case of withdrawal from the community.[16]

Communalism, once firmly established, was in time to assume a weight that even Metz himself did not anticipate. "As truly as I live says the Lord, it is at no time my will to dissolve the ties of community." Communalism became part of the religious myth, sanctified and protected by it. When in the 1920s it was clear to many that a break from communalism was unavoidable, community debates show the rear guard reminding the pro-Change faction that "there shall come eternal disgrace, shame, and disfavor upon those who cause [the community's dissolution]." As we shall see in the following chapters, communalism came to permeate every aspect of colony life. By demanding greater commitment to community, it helped foster it. When in future years that commitment had to be reexamined, it acted as a powerful if failing brake on change. Today, paradoxically, it is the communal aspect—now history—that most powerfully draws tourists into a community that formerly shunned outsiders.

But that was far in the future. The early Ebenezer residents eagerly set about adding to their religion a political and economic structure. Developing these structures has often proved difficult for communal groups, especially when egalitarianism is prized. First, authority must be established, if not in one or several persons or offices, then in some clearly delineated principle and political process. Failure to accomplish this is counted among the many causes of New Harmony's demise, and sociologist Rosabeth Kanter also sees the "do your own thing" ethic as leading to the early end of many a 1960s commune.[17] Whatever egalitarianism was to be found in pietist thought did not prevent the Inspirationists from vesting authority in the person of the *Werkzeug*. At Ebenezer and later in Iowa political authority grew to be virtually synonymous with religious authority. *Werkzeug*, trustees, and elders had different tasks, powers, and responsibilities but functioned in a complementary rather than competitive manner.

During the height of Amana's existence, Metz—more than Heinemann-Landmann, who outlived him—was the real and acknowledged leader, arranging both the first move from Germany to Ebenezer and the second move to Iowa. Orchestrating the combination of practical organization with spiritual direction, he was primarily responsible for developing the communal structure of the group. Metz was more patient, more generous, and more forgiving than Landmann, whose *Bezeughungen* (testimonies) were harsher, especially during her later years, and who was never considered fully Metz's equal, either before or after his death.[18]

Under the *Werkzeug* was the board of trustees. Responsible for the major temporal affairs of the community, it comprised thirteen elders elected yearly (though once elected they tended to maintain their positions). Trustees would decide on such issues as the economic course of the Amanas and their relationship with the outside world. Under the trustees were the village elders. These men were responsible both for the spiritual well-being of their villages and for the comparatively minor day-to-day practical decisions. For the average resident, the elders were the most immediate figures of authority. They decided who could marry whom, who could work at what job, who would travel to the outside when and for what purpose, and who would receive what punishment for what indiscretion. Considerable power was also held by the general managers of each major economic enterprise, including the farms, the mills, and the shops. Since trustees had to have at least some economic training and awareness, many were both managers and elders.

In his dissertation Jonathan Andelson studied the origins of the institution of the elders and came to some rather interesting conclusions. The first elders named by Krausert shortly after the group's revival in the early 1800s, while it was still deeply involved in political struggle with the old leadership, tended to be former elders who had accepted the renewed faith. The first named by Metz tended to be close personal friends. In the years preceding the move to the United States, wealthy recruits were likely to be named as elders, presumably as one means of rewarding them for their financial contributions. After the move those who had been with the group in Germany were more likely to be named than were more recent joiners. Certain family names appeared as elders generation after generation: others never made the list.[19]

Indeed, this "aristocracy of elders" nascent in the early Ebenezer days might have served as warning to the rank and file that under the proposed communalism some were created more equal than others. This leadership structure had been legitimated not just by the inequalities brought into the sect from the secular world—differences in money and talent—but also by the divine word of inspiration and further injunctions of the theology: "To obey without reasoning God, and through God, our superiors." The myth legitimated the politics: to fight against it would be equivalent, for the believer, to taking on both heaven and city hall. Nonetheless, this built-in inequality in a society that espoused absolute equality and self-surrender was a critical flaw that would not go forever unnoticed.

Besides their political leadership, it also fell to the trustees to mold the residents into a well-oiled economic system. At the outset they faced questions and difficulties common to many organizers of alternative societies. How would they put to work, feed, clothe, and shelter all the people? How would they see that the children were educated and socialized into community values? What would be their relation to outsiders? Would they sell to them or shun them, close themselves off or deal on the open market?

In her comparison of communal societies, Rosabeth Kanter outlines three broad forms that the resolution of these questions may assume. A communal group may opt for self-sufficiency, aiming to produce all their food, tools, clothing, and other necessities of life. Many groups favor this form because of the problems seen to stem from any interaction with the outside world. A second resolution is specialization, gearing communal efforts toward one or two products that can be sold on the outside to buy other needed products. Oneida, renowned for its silver and its animal traps, is a good example. A third form the solution may take is attempting to live within—and off—dominant society, a solution attempted by a number of urban communes.[20]

Among the Inspirationists, the economic organization that emerged was developed on the model of the old German social order they had left behind—as, in fact, had Germany herself. The life and economy of each of the seven Amana villages was based on considerable self-sufficiency, but the community as a whole also developed several items for trade on the outside. This economy was based on a highly structured assignment of tasks. When a boy finished school the elders would decide his occupation, usually a far from arbitrary decision that took into account the boy's own preferences as well as the recommendation of any adult he might already have worked with. A handful of boys would be sent to the outside for further education, but usually only when it became apparent that their particular village would be needing a doctor or teacher. Most boys were assigned to work in the fields, at a skilled trade, or in the mills, with a certain flexibility built into the system so that men and jobs could be switched, especially at harvesttime. Amana did not favor the deliberate rotation of jobs as did the Shakers, having no special belief that it was more rewarding to be skilled at a number of jobs than at one. Agriculture involved the largest number of men, and major crops included rye, barley, oats, corn, potatoes, and onions. There was also livestock to tend, and the community in time grew famous for its meat products.

The community very early struck a balance between agriculture and industry. While the group was still in Germany it had rented mills and factories for its skilled tradesmen. Spinning machines were provided for the weavers, providing the basis for an eventual woolen industry. There were also a soap works and a gristmill.[21]

Unlike the boys, the girls could have little cause for speculation about their work as adults. For girls and women, the major work was in the communal kitchens and gardens, with married women usually working in the gardens and unmarried ones in the kitchens. Originally all members ate in the kitchen houses except the ill, for whom a home basket was prepared, and all sat in silence, men and women at separate tables. Each kitchen house served approximately forty. As in the other branches of the economy, the kitchen was under the direction of a supervisor, the kitchen boss, aided by her assistants. Much of the communal activity centered on the kitchen, and the boss was its focus. Women too old for heavy kitchen work or gardening might work in the preschool or possibly teach knitting to the children. All women and girls also spent any spare minute engaged in "fancywork"— intricate knitting, crochet-work, or embroidery.[22]

VIEWS FROM THE OUTSIDE

Descriptions of early Ebenezer life are scarce, but one rather charming account from a visit by two Shaker men in 1846 provides an outsider's impressions of the settlement and its people:

We hired a horse and wagon at the livery stables in Buffalo on Wednesday, August 12, 1846. We left the city at about half past nine o'clock AM. Having been informed before we left that it was three miles to the settlement we expected to reach it in a short time. After we had driven about two miles we asked a man how far it was to the German settlement. He told us it was about three miles. We drove on a while longer and inquired again and were informed that it was five miles. We began to think we could not make the road any shorter by inquiring for the distance increased every time we asked and we nearly despaired of ever finding the mysterious people. However, we drove on till we came to a road turning to the left. This we were directed to take. We did so, and after a few minutes drive we came to a Dutch gate across our road. This we opened, passed through and closed again, and then drove fording a brook of considerable size and then passed another gate as before. We were now in fair sight of their first village which consisted of about forty dwellings of two stories averaging 35 × 45 feet on the base, according to my judgment. These dwellings were painted white on the outside but were left the common wood color inside. There were many barns and outbuildings, besides two saw mills and a large factory. . . .

We halted before a conspicuous-looking house. All was still and quiet throughout the village. We went to the door, knocked and an elderly man came to the door. We asked whether Charles Mayer was at home. The man could not understand or speak English. He stepped away and presently a young woman appeared at the door, about the age of 23, wearing a plain dress and a cheerful smiling countenance. We asked whether we could see Charles, to which she replied in broken English that he was then in a meeting but we could see him in half an hour. . . .

While we were waiting for their meeting to close we heard them sing a lengthy song in four parts. The singing was so smooth that I positively believed they had instrumental music but afterwards heard they make no use of musical instruments. . . .

After we had conversed a while with Charles, four of their elders came in to see us. We shook hands with the compliment of a graceful bow and pleasant smiles. Their appearance, dress and actions were common, easy, and firm. We held some conversation with the elders through Charles, the interpreter, of living pure and holy lives and of giving all glory to God.

About noon there came an elderly sister to the room with a basket of food steaming hot, consisting of a dish of milk porridge and bread, fried ham, spoon cakes fried in fat rich with eggs, bread and butter, plum preserves, tea, milk and sugar and a queer dish of mixed vegetables consisting of cucumbers, onions, milk and pepper, all mixed together. After dinner the elders who had left the room except for Charles came in and sat down, and through the interpreter we had some more talk with them.[23]

Other more typical visitors from the Buffalo area were particularly struck by the colonists' system of communal work. One county history tells us that "the sight of the great gangs of men and women, fifty to a hundred, engaged in the ordinary avocations of a farm, was something entirely new to the eyes of Erie county people." Even more striking to these outsiders was the harvest scene of "a row, half mile long, of women, a few yards apart, reaping with sickles the grain of the community."[24] As would often be the case in later years, outsiders misperceived the Inspirationist religion, believing it akin to that of the Friends, with the *Werkzeug* simply leading the others in speaking out in church. And, while their economic and political structure was far from well understood by their neighbors, the Ebenezer Inspirationists do seem to have garnered a modicum of respect for both, as the following account suggests:

The State authorities once sent a circular to the trustees as they did to the other local officials, asking how many paupers there were among them, how many crimes and misdemeanors had been committed in a specified time, with other similar questions. The reply was brief and simple: there were no paupers among them; none of them had ever received any relief from the civil authorities; none of them had, so far as was known, committed any crime or misdemeanor, and none of them had ever had a law suit, either with another member or an outsider. One or two disputes with Americans had been settled by the trustees without suit.[25]

"It should be added," the report went on, "that everything produced by the community was of the best quality and was always found to be strictly as recommended."[26]

THREATS TO COMMUNITY

Underneath the calm exterior, however, serious problems rankled, problems that threatened the very existence of the communal order. For one, it appears that both the Indians who supposedly sold the land and the Inspirationists who bought and settled it had been ill handled by an unscrupulous land company. One account states that in 1838 the Ogden Company obtained "a doubtful conveyance" of the Seneca reservation for the sum of $202,000. What was particularly doubtful, as revealed by the investigation that followed, was a long trail of bribery and corruption, including "shameful methods . . . of intoxication" used in obtaining the signatures of Indians who in any case were not recognized chieftains. Public indignation was reportedly so great that at first the land company did not try to enforce its claim, but by 1842 it had succeeded in obtaining the Buffalo Creek and Tonawanda reservations. Most of the Indians slowly left, some for other parts of western New York, others to move farther west. While the report considered their departure "a distinct advantage for the city, for soon a different class, a worthy class of neighbor [speaking of the Inspirationists] occupied land in the former reservation," purchasing this legally entangled land was a distinct disadvantage to the colonists themselves. Some Indians stayed on until 1846, when the government sided with the Inspirationists and forced the last of them to move on toward a new reservation.[27]

Unfortunate as this all was, the Indian problem was minor compared with the threats from the other white settlers and especially from the growing city of Buffalo. Buffalo residents expressed a normal curiosity about their strange neighbors, and some of the Inspirationists were equally curious about the people of Buffalo. The population explosion this city experienced in connection with the easy transportation west provided by the Erie Canal had predictable effects on social life. In the late 1830s Buffalo was already experiencing a number of urban problems: crime, drunkenness, squalor—social disorganization of every brand.[28] It was already developing into a true city, with all the excitement and, for Inspirationists, all the forbidden temptations. Since Ebenezer did not try to enforce total isolation and economic self-sufficiency, it was inevitable that the moral boundaries of city and settlement would soon rub against each other. Tourists drove their horses and buggies through the small Ebenezer villages, and villagers were interested in what they saw of the outside. Acts of deviance large and small became so common that on one occasion Metz was inspired to proclaim:

It should be announced in Ober that it is a fat pit to death, and that it has become a valley of deviants in Nieder. They run off to the city to make love, to have intercourse with the untrue and deviant, with the world so that there is no longer difference. And here it is too in the same degree and measure. Therefore, it has become an abomination before the Lord.[29]

A second problem prominent in this period was a "creeping materialism" among the members—and not just the young. Some in particular were finding business activities for private profit more rewarding than those leading to communal gain. Even more serious, however, this interaction with the outside was effecting a decline in religious enthusiasm. Among the various forms of misconduct created by the too-close presence of the outside world, this was "the subtlest form, the most difficult to deal with, and possibly the most dangerous."[30]

But there were other forces undermining the community, affecting not just the Inspirationists but neighboring villagers and farmers. To some extent the social change the Inspirationists had fled in Germany had caught up with them in New York. Here too artisanal work was being undermined by industrialization. Buffalo was growing as an industrial center at the expense of the surrounding rural area, forcing a modernization in agriculture that made some men successes, but created more failures.[31] The increase in population and the rise in land values led to substantial land hunger, and the Inspirationists found their nine thousand acres (their leaders having already made additional purchases) too few to support their twelve hundred members and their coffers inadequate to purchase more land at the new high prices.[32] There were also political uncertainties. One account suggests in somewhat general terms that "public opinion . . . looked unfavorably on a system so contrary to all American ideas" and, more specifically, that "it was considered doubtful whether their charter would be renewed."[33] Hence, like many other New York State residents, the Inspirationists began looking farther west. Once again the political decision to move was legitimated by Metz's inspiration, which in 1854 directed that several men be sent out in search of new land. The party first looked at Kansas, but they saw little there to interest them and so returned. Then a second small party, in December of that year, left to assess possibilities in Iowa. They discovered a large and fertile tract on the Iowa River in Iowa County, containing both timberland and pastureland with nearby sandstone deposits and a river that could be harnessed to power their mills. The Mesquakie Indian claim had expired in 1843, so there appeared to be no problem with conflicting rights. In 1854 there were still only a few settlers who would have to be bought out so that a continuous tract could be pieced together. This time the leaders made certain to purchase enough land—twenty-six thousand acres as contrasted to the original five thousand at Ebenezer, most of it bought directly from the government and far enough away from city lights to ensure that their followers would find their only illumination through inspiration.

And for a time this would succeed.

Iowa County, Iowa

CHAPTER 3

Iɴ the 1850s Iowa was experiencing its first great decade of settlement. Declared a state only in 1846, now in the early fifties Iowa was welcoming migrants from the South, from the middle Atlantic states, and increasingly from the Northeast. Immigrants from Germany, Ireland, England, France, and Scandinavia were arriving, many of them encouraged by guidebooks in their native languages telling of the wondrously fertile soil and great economic opportunities available in this new state. Indeed, of all these new settlers only one group, the freed blacks, would receive less than an enthusiastic welcome.[1]

In the mid-1850s the United States was edging toward civil war, debating slavery, abolition, and states' rights. Early Iowans took a keen interest in these debates, especially those being carried on immediately to the southwest in Kansas and Nebraska. While many residents were antislavery,[2] the Inspirationists themselves mostly sought to keep out of politics and avoided military service even if it meant paying for replacements, a stance dictated by their traditional pacifism. What they *did* want was separation from the affairs of the world, political and otherwise—the time and space to re-create the integrated community life they had known in Germany and experimented with in Ebenezer. By choosing this still-new state of Iowa they would for a time succeed in controlling, or at least mediating, the impact of the outside world on their villages.

Iowa was then primarily a state of farmers, along with the usual artisans, shopkeepers, and professionals. Its only major industries, logically enough, manufactured farm equipment. There were, in addition, lumber companies and sawmills, plus the basis for what was to be a major meat-packing industry.[3] In 1852 the population stood at 229,000; by 1854 it had increased to 326,500. While in 1850–54 the population increased by an average of 40,000 each year, after 1854 it surged, reaching 674,913 in 1860. With this surge in population the sources of migration changed, and after 1854 the Northeast replaced the South as the major source of new settlers.[4]

Among the foreign immigrants, Germans predominated. Large numbers of Germans settled the towns along the Mississippi, in Davenport, Burlington, Muscatine, and Dubuque. They arrived in families and in large groups, sometimes whole villages. Isolated families and single people usually stayed in cities or close to settled areas; the groups often pushed farther inland to find the large tracts their numbers demanded. In 1850 one group of Germans attempted to establish a socialist colony, "Communia," in Clayton County, while others simply attempted to re-create their villages of origin. One of the most noteworthy colonies was created by a Dutch land company whose 884 members settled the town of Pella in 1850.[5] The staying power of such communities was often linked to a strong church or to a shared provincial background yielding a homogeneous population,[6] and indeed such social control and shared experience served to hold the Amana community together through the early building period.

The Society of True Inspiration chose to look inland for a tract large enough to hold its approximately twelve hundred members. The scouting party discovered a fertile river valley some twenty miles west of Iowa City. No train yet extended that far, though there was talk that rails would eventually be laid out to Marengo, the county seat. Thus, after having traveled across the Great Lakes by steamer and down from Chicago to Rock Island by rail, then crossing the Mississippi, the early Inspirationists would have to suffer the last leg of their long journey in oxcarts. The view that greeted them at their destination, however, would have been worth it.[7]

The trustees had managed to piece together—partly by buying out the early settlers, partly by buying direct from the government—a tract of some twenty-six thousand acres comprising gentle hills, timberland, and fields, all divided by the Iowa River, which curved gently through its center. There were small hills on which to build villages, saving the best land for fields of oats, barley, onions, and corn. The leaders also bought the small village of Homestead from its owners in hopes that it would become a stop on the railway, which in time it did. Sandstone pits nearby would yield material for houses and churches. The site, in short, had everything—but most of all it provided isolation.

The Inspirationists were not the only communal group to prize such separation from the world. Some scholars have argued that the frontier itself is integrally connected with the history of utopianism in America because of the number of utopias that were founded along its ever-changing borders.[8] Certainly Iowa attracted its share of religious dissenters and utopia-seekers. Among the best known are the Amish, some of whom left their homes in Pennsylvania and Ohio in the late 1840s and 1850s to build new communities at a number of Iowa sites, including Kalona, not far from Iowa City.[9] Also, in one of the sadder chapters of utopian history, a group of Icarians migrated from France to Texas, where they were deceived regarding their purchase of land and so had to push on to the old Mormon site at Nauvoo, Illinois. There they stayed only briefly before making their final trek to Corning, Iowa, where they stuck it out, despite severe economic deprivation and serious schism within their ranks, from 1856 to 1870. While their success was limited, they did at least represent a serious attempt to turn the ideas of Etienne Cabet into reality on the Iowa frontier.[10]

The America that encountered such foreign groups as the Icarians and the Inspirationists was in the 1850s still a pioneer society in which many were land rich but few were money rich.[11] One early account of life in the river city of Davenport tells of widespread speculation not only in land but in crops, of notes written in the fall that were not considered due until the spring because of the shortage of money, most of which seemed to be flowing in and out of wildcat banks in Nebraska. Boats bringing immigrants made their way up the Mississippi, their cargo welcome except when rumors of cholera circulated.[12]

But Davenport and other river cities represented civilization compared with life in the interior. One account of a settler who arrived in Iowa County in 1853 describes the land as "newly settled and with very few improvements, abounding in large stretches of prairie and considerable bodies of timber." The few houses were one-story log cabins, their inhabitants mostly from Ohio, Kentucky, or Tennessee, plus a few from the eastern states and some from European countries, especially the British Isles and Germany. "These pioneers were hustlers," wrote the settler, "for it was invariably a case of 'root hog or die'":

Money was very scarce. Consequently, every thing was very cheap. Dressed pork sold from $1.75 to $2.00 per hundred and cut corn was 10 cents per bushel. . . . There were no mills in the county and the nearest one outside was at Iowa City. Sometimes the pioneers would have to wait ten days or two weeks to get their grist: and again the water would come up in the rivers and compel them to wait at home until fording was possible.[13]

As for the town that would become the county seat, the settler wrote:

When I came to Iowa County there were no places that could be called a town, without stretching the imagination considerably. Marengo was a small place, consisting of but fourteen dwellings, two stores, a blacksmith shop, one hotel, one 1½ story loghouse. There were but three dwellings built of anything but logs. There was a small post office, a stage station and a saloon.[14]

Yet county, like state, experienced the 1850s as the decade of settlement, a process aided in no small measure by the Inspirationists' move (table 1). Many of the Society's neighbors were also Germans, but, as we shall see, relations between the two groups would not always be *gemütlich*. In one sense the Amana residents had an advantage over their neighbors in these early days because the group had already worked out their political and economic structure, first on the German estates, then in a trial run in New York State. Indeed, the Society's rapid and successful establishment in Iowa was due in no small measure to the generally unsettled character of the surrounding society, to the

Table 1: Population of Iowa County, Iowa

Period	Population	Period	Population
1847	435	1875	18,456
1850	822	1880	19,221
1854	2,307	1885	18,190
1856	4,873	1890	18,270
1860	8,029	1895	18,964
1865	10,258	1900	19,544
1870	16,644	1905	18,977

Source: James C. Dinwiddie, *A History of Iowa County, Iowa, and Its People* (Chicago: S. J. Clarke, 1915).

fact that American society, like Amana itself, was in the process of building communities. Amana's decline as a communal society, in turn, would reflect the penetration of community by society, the changing locus and scale of political and economic decision making.[15]

But that was far in the future. In the 1850s and 1860s the Iowa pioneers were still building their communities and their social life, and one of their major concerns was religious life. One of the earliest forms this concern took was the Methodist camp meetings that were held periodically throughout the rural areas. Such meetings were social as well as religious events and often generated enthusiastic response:

At an early date the Methodists established a camp on the banks of Honey Creek . . . and meetings were held there annually, each lasting from one to two weeks. . . . There would be ministers here from all over the country, and after several days preaching, exhorting, and shouting— each taking turns, never giving the people a chance to breathe—they would arouse their audience to a frenzy of religious enthusiasm. . . . Some would fall as if in a fit, some would become rigid as a gun barrel, some would become unconscious for hours, then arouse themselves and shoutingly proclaim that they had seen visions of the kingdom of heaven.[16]

Efforts were also being made to establish regular congregations, and the traveling missionary was the key to this effort. In the early 1850s one Lutheran missionary from Rock Island, Illinois, traveled the county. "He was common and daring, defied weather and storms, in fact was equal to the occasion. . . . He visited one settlement every three or four weeks. The second time he brought a violin with him to accompany the singing. At another time he brought a harmonica. People were as much pleased with this as with a large organ. Later he traveled with a horse, which was quite an improvement. In 1860 he got married."[17] Churches of all denominations, but primarily Lutheran, Presbyterian, Methodist, and Baptist, were organized as new immigrants arrived. Such churches and their ministers played a leading role in small towns throughout the Midwest and West, helping both in establishing the communities and in integrating newcomers into the social and moral order.[18] Their role and importance were not unlike those of the Amana church and elders, though the basis of their authority and the structure of their societies differed.

Soon, however, these far-flung settlements grew into respectable small towns with pretensions toward civilization. The county seat of Iowa County received its impressive name of Marengo when three men, appointed by the legislature in 1844 to locate the county seat, drove out to that vicinity, where they reportedly came across one Robert McKee mowing grass, "a well-filled jug in his wagon." After much frequenting of the jug, the men decided this had to be the place. One of them tore off his red shirt-tail and hoisted it on a pole while another christened the site "Marengo," since it "bore a strong resemblance to the plains of Marengo in Italy where Napoleon won a great battle from the Austrian troops."[19]

Signs of civilization followed one after the other. The first term of court was held in 1846, the town officially laid out and constructed in 1847. The first newspaper appeared in 1856 and, predictably, the first delinquent tax list in 1857. The first recorded discussion of female suffrage took place in 1854. In 1860 Marengo was connected to the railroad, and its early industries—brick and tile works, woolen mills, and gristmills—were established. In 1868 a "severe temperance wave" swept through town, and Clara Barton of the American Red Cross paid a visit. Shade trees were planted. Yet all was not law and order. Indians still made their way back to their former land, the sheriff periodically seized a still, and violent accidents and death were a daily part of life.[20]

By the late 1860s the Society of True Inspiration was well established in its new home. Visitors to the community during this period were few. The writer/journalist Charles Nordhoff, as part of his research on communal societies, stayed in Amana in 1875 and found it prospering with some 1,450 members. The members had dug a seven-mile millrace that wound throughout their land providing power for the woolen mills, sawmills, and gristmills. Each village had one major road through its center. Most dwelling houses faced onto this road, with the kitchen houses and small sheds behind them. Each village also contained a general store, a small inn for visitors, shoemaker, tailor, and carpenter shops, and, except for East Amana, some sort of mill. The individual dwellings, which Nordhoff misperceived as housing only one family each, were

well-built, of brick, stone, or wood, very plain, each with a sufficient garden, but most standing immediately on the street. They use no paint, believing that wood lasts as well without. There is usually a narrow sidewalk of boards or bricks and the schoolhouse and church are notable buildings only because of their greater size. Like the Quakers, they abhor "steeple-houses," and their church architecture is of the plainest.[21]

A newspaper article appearing about 1900 described the typical interior of an Inspirationist house as follows:

Most of the houses are a series of bedrooms and parlors. The floors are covered with black carpet striped in red and a touch of yellow. Little mats of woven corn husks are placed in front of the doors.

The massive furniture, all made in Amana, makes the filled rooms look small, although in reality they are of average size. Many handmade flowers, framed in glass, hang on the walls. The shining tables are covered with large, fine knit or crocheted doilies. Many finely carved trinkets, some in the shape of dogs and other domestic animals, adorn the tables. Numerous stools are placed regularly about their rooms. The people have a taste for bright and fancy tightly stuffed pillows, mostly in flower designs. They stand these in corners and at the back of chairs.

The walls of the homes and churches are tinted in a light blue. . . .

Every place the appearance of bright cleanliness prevails. Each family has at least one fine clock of which it is very proud.[22]

The first recorded notice by the press in Iowa of the colony appeared in the nearby *Cedar Rapids Gazette* in an article published 1 October 1883, under the heading "An Iowa Commune: History and Habits of the Amana Society in Iowa." Although largely favorable—"They are a thoroughly honest people, whatever they do is well done"—the article was filled with inaccuracies. It confused the Inspirationist doctrine and practice with those of the Quakers, relating that, while the service was conducted by a leader, "the speaking is done by different individuals as the spirit moves them." The marriage ceremony was also considered to be "precisely like that of the Quakers." Emphasizing the high quality of Amana cotton and woolen goods, the *Gazette* confidently informed its readers that "the Society is immensely wealthy and has no need for money." With reports like that, no wonder many of Amana's neighbors, individual farmers struggling to make ends meet on land that was not always their own, envied the apparently secure life communalism provided.

Yet by the time this report appeared in 1883 many scholars would say the heyday of communalism was already well past. Certainly the Shakers had suffered massive declines in numbers and fortunes, and Oneida had already moved from commune to corporation. However, as Robert Fogarty has demonstrated, throughout the post–Civil War period at least some people continued to see communalism as a viable alternative to capitalism. Attempts at forming such alternative societies fell largely into three broad categories: cooperative colonizers aiming to change behaviors and improve morality primarily through economic cooperation; political pragmatists often finding in socialism the answers to modern-day ills; and charismatic perfectionists who believed that perfection could be reached on earth, at least within their own communities. In this period of supposed decline, at least seventeen communal societies were organized during the decade of the 1870s, another fifteen during the 1880s, and thirty-six in the 1890s, and at least twenty-two more projects were initiated between 1900 and 1919.[23] Clearly, as Fogarty points out, arguments that "it wouldn't work" or that "it had been tried before" didn't hold back would-be communards in the latter half of the nineteenth century.[24]

And in Amana, despite certain difficulties predictable and otherwise and some degree of social conflict, communalism was indeed working.

Amana Social Life and Social Control

CHAPTER 4

To make a success of any communal society, members must face certain problems, problems that Rosabeth Kanter has correctly identified as centering on the issue of commitment. Where, in short, does individual allegiance belong? To the individual's own personhood and will? To the family? Or to the community as a whole? To add weight to the side of community, many communal attempts have adopted one or more of what Kanter calls "commitment mechanisms." These mechanisms include an emphasis on sacrifice through various forms of abstinence, such as abstinence from sex, alcohol, and tobacco. Members are also encouraged to invest in the community, often giving up personal goods and money as well as time and energy. Various forms of renunciation—of one's earlier life, family and friends, and the outside world—also serve to increase commitment, as does the communal structure itself, with its emphasis on building communion through shared group characteristics, shared work and ownership of property, and important group rituals. Through mortification, another mechanism, the individual ego is reduced in significance compared with the group. This can be accomplished through confession, mutual criticism, or sanctions against displays of individual will. Finally, transcendence provides a positive force for commitment insofar as it is through group membership that the individual seeks to reach a higher spiritual goal or effect a greater social good. This experience of transcendence can be encouraged through endowing certain individuals within the group with awe-inspiring qualities, through developing a sense of magic and mystery, through the conversion experience, or through appeal to group tradition. As Kanter notes, Amana is a good example of a communal society that continued to maintain its membership and structure in part because it incorporated many of these commitment mechanisms.[1]

While much of Amana social structure worked to instill a sense of community, there remained points of tension between individuals and families, families and community, and community and American society. To study both the process through which the individual would be socialized into group identity and social roles and also the points of tension and conflict that remained, let us follow the lifetime of a hypothetical Inspirationist born in the late nineteenth century. What follows is a composite picture of what it was like to grow up in and become part of Amana, based largely on interviews with elderly Amana members. Their reminiscences describe the period 1900–1920. The second half of the chapter covers a broader time period in describing the maintenance of boundaries between community and American society, moving from the early years of Iowa settlement through the 1890s up to the 1920s.

CHILDHOOD

The Inspirationist child would likely be brought into the world by a midwife, one of the older women of the village who was often a friend or relative of the mother, or possibly by one of the few Amana doctors who had been sent outside the community for his training. The parents would then decide on a name, often through a politic balancing of names drawn from one side of the family with those drawn from the other. The mother would be freed from communal labor for two years to look after the newborn member.

The child's world encompassed first the extended family, then the particular village, and only then, at somewhat of a distance, the larger reality of the Society of True Inspiration. From the child's earliest days it was the richness of the extended family that formed a comfortable surround, providing at once a broad view of human nature and a network of emotional resources for support, criticism, and guidance. Grandparents and parents often shared the same house, and aunts and uncles were sure to live close by. All relatives and even neighbors made socializing the young child their proper business, instructing him or her in community values of work, thrift, and what was termed *Gelassenheit*—the calm exterior, the "self-forgetting" nature demanded of those who live and work closely together. Besides setting an example by their own behavior and giving frequent admonition and praise, many adults relied on such didactic tools as children's books published in German, perhaps the best known of which concerned a character called "der Struwwelpeter," a negative example if there ever was one. Der Struwwelpeter refused to comb his hair; birds came to nest in it. He refused to cut his nails; he sat on them and bled to death. He laughed at a little black boy; three old men dunked him in a vat of boiling molasses, and he emerged darker than the boy he laughed at. Dr. Spock's techniques, in short, were not favored by a group that aimed at curbing individual will and developing communal responsibility. Yet the Amana child's world was not as harsh as was der Struwwelpeter's. This wide circle of relatives was the source not only of occasional scoldings but of unexpected treats. One man who grew up in the early 1900s remembers such a benevolent relative: "My grandfather Friedrich was a good egg. And he liked to have a drink. It didn't take much. When he had a drink, he would give us the coupon book and tell us to go and buy ourselves some candy." The coupon book was part of the Amana system of rationing; the coupons could be redeemed for items at the village store, and the total was carefully decided by the trustees on the basis of family size and allotted annually.[2] Few mothers would have approved of these precious coupons being spent on candy.

When the mother returned to kitchen or garden work this extended circle of relatives could be counted on for child care. Siblings, aunts, uncles, grandparents—all were on call, though again the sense of family or communal responsibility did not always rule over individual design. One woman, the baby of the family, recalls that if her mother was out and her sisters didn't want to take care of her they would often send her next door to her grandmother's: "I remember once, an outsider boy who was dating my sister paid me a whole dime to go next door. That was a lot of money. I would have gone for a penny."

Cracks in the communal wall? Indeed, it was against such worldly influences as outsider boys with their ready dimes that older members had to be continually on guard in socializing the young. Temptation to individual desire or distinction cropped up constantly, and members varied in temperament, motivation, and deportment. One still-sprightly woman well recalls her mischievous youth and the trouble she got into from a disapproving aunt:

Louise was her favorite. But me! I was *die Schlimmste!* How do you say that in English? The rotten apple in the bunch! I always went around with Elizabeth and Katherine, who were older than me, and Aunt Lena thought I was up to no good, that I should be with girls my own age. And then one day I'll never forget, I wore a purple ribbon in my hair to the kitchens. I had on a purple dress, and I wore a purple ribbon. She just about jumped out of her skin, the things she said about me.

Aunt Lena would come to visit us quite often, and her grandniece Katherine would run ahead warning us that she was on her way so we could hide anything she wouldn't approve of. Once she came to complain about us to her sister, our Grandmother, because we had been taking the old colored pillowcases and making aprons, and we were sitting doing our fancywork on the other side of the door and we heard her say these terrible things about us and ask Grandmother what she was going to do about us. Grandmother just said, "Oh, let them be!"

The extended family was thus not simply a valuable resource. It was a rich, if occasionally oppressive, environment in a society in which everyone knew, and cared about, everyone else's business.

SCHOOLING

The family was not the only environment to which the young child was exposed. When the mother returned to work the child would be sent to the *Kinderschule*, or child-care center, run by two of the older women who could no longer work in the communal kitchens or gardens. In the *Kinderschule* the child would join others of the same age in playing with toys made by cabinetmakers or sewn by the women. The star attraction of each schoolyard would be a large swing with seats on two sides. There was little attempt to teach skills such as the alphabet or counting until children began regular school at age five. Then the emphasis was on the dual purposes of moral training and instruction in some skill, along with basic reading and writing. For the first purpose the schools relied heavily on the text *Children's Voices* (*Kinder-Stimme*), which contained a detailed list of rules and regulations, including some of the following:

Do not seek your desires and ambitions in great knowledge and understanding, but rather in self-negation and self-denial.

If you feel a living impulse in your soul to seek quiet seclusion and meditation for intercourse with God in prayer, by all means do not disregard it. For the gate of love then stands open to you.

The smaller you are in your own eyes the better can the grace of God reveal itself in you.

In addition to these precepts children were responsible for knowing and following the "Sixty-six Rules for the Conduct of Children," which included such admonitions as:

Be quiet while at the table, unless you are asked a question; the prattle of children while eating is a grave lack of manners.

Show yourself kind and peaceable toward your fellow pupils, do not kick them, or make them dirty with your shoe or in some other manner; call them no bad names, and behave yourself always toward them as you wish that they should behave toward you.

When going home avoid all noise and jumping, and walk quietly and mannerly.[3]

To emphasize the practical skills without neglecting necessary basics, the Amana society separated the school day into three parts. First came the *Lehrschule*, for the basics of reading, writing, and numbers, followed by the *Spielstunde*, or play hour, after which came the *Arbeitschule*, when manual training, trades, and crafts were taught. In the wintertime the young boys and girls would learn to knit, while the older boys learned a trade and the older girls cleared up the schoolhouse or helped with the knitting. In the summer all were likely to help with the harvest. The school hours were long, since men and women alike were out working all day, and there were no extended vacation periods.[4]

Assuming satisfactory progress, the child would finish school at age fourteen, then take up the work that would be his or her life's assignment within the community. In their task of placing the school leaver firmly within the adult economic structure, the village elders had a considerable body of information available. They would consider family background and standing: a carpenter's son might well follow his father in the craft; a farmworker's son would most likely also work on the village farm. The elders could consider performance at school and demonstrated aptitudes. They might also examine the young member's religious status. In Amana this abstract concept had one concrete indicator. You knew where you stood in God's eyes by where you sat in his church.

CHURCH INSTRUCTION

The church building itself was plain, with a brick or sandstone exterior and whitewashed walls and plain pine benches inside. The row of elders sat in front on a bench facing the congregation, and the presiding elder for the day sat at a small cloth-covered table.

There were three congregations, or *Versammlungen*: one for the children, one for the young adults, one for the older people. Most church meetings would be attended by all congregations, with seating determined by age, the older members having the honor of sitting farther back. Once or twice a week each congregation met separately, and for some purposes, such as the *Liebesmahl* (Lord's Supper) celebration, four *Versammlungen* would be identified, the fourth for the young children. Normally a child would enter the church and sit in the first row in the children's congregation when he or she turned seven. Assuming good behavior, the child would move back month by month, year by year, until it was time to graduate to the next *Versammlung*, where the process would repeat itself. Good behavior, however, was often too much to assume. A common indiscretion that our child of the early 1900s might well have committed was playing baseball, or watching it. A woman now in her early seventies remembers a time when:

The two of us girls went down to watch the baseball game. The Amana boys were playing an outsider team. Of course it was illegal, the playing and the watching, and we knew we would be excommunicated for at least several weeks if we were caught. But we took the chance. And we were caught. I suppose we felt we were doing something very wicked.

Offenders like these players and spectators might be locked out of church altogether ("excommunicated") for a given period.

With such stern control through school and church, one might conclude that an Amana childhood was dull indeed. But current residents remember it differently and recall pleasant times playing with their friends in orchards and woods, alongside the mill-race or on backyard swings, now priding themselves on how "we made our own fun." Sometimes grandparents would get involved in this lighter side of socializing the young.

Well, we didn't have much time left over for fun, but we did have a couple hours on Sunday. We would all sit around and sing German songs— have a songfest. Grandpa and Grandma would tell stories about Germany—when we were little we knew more about Germany than our own country. Or sometimes Grandpa would play a game with us, "Going to Germany."

I remember how Grandma would always talk about how they had all taken the train from Ebenezer, and how they passed through "To'ledo." She always gave it the German pronunciation "To'ledo."

Grandparents symbolized the original religious devotion on which the Amana Colonies were built.

We used to have what grandma called the "Twilight Hour." Every day at that time she would ask us if we had been good, if our activities that day had brought us closer to or further from God.

On Saturday afternoon too, starting at 12:30, she would refuse to work. She needed that time, she said, to get ready for Sunday. She thought what you did to get ready for Sunday was more important than what you did on Sunday itself. She would sit for several hours and silently review her whole week. She would never ask us to do it, or speak out loud, but we knew she was doing it for herself.

SPECIAL OCCASIONS

Within this homogeneous community exotic outsiders would occasionally visit, breaking the monotony of the well-ordered life. A woman of West Amana remembers the excitement that visiting Indians and gypsies provided:

I remember the Indians would come in the summer down from Tama where they had their reservation, and West Amana would be the first of the Amanas they would hit. We used to give them fresh bread, and they would give us beads in exchange. We never spoke. We would hold it out to them and smile. We weren't afraid. The Indians never stole anything.

The gypsies stole. They would steal anything that wasn't nailed down. Whenever the gypsies came, my sisters would watch over me carefully. It was Uncle Heinrich who told me never to be afraid of gypsies, for he said if they stole me at night, when it came to be morning and they saw what they had gotten they would always return me.

Hoboes too would make the Amanas a sure stop on their travels. One woman in South Amana stressed that the hoboes had somehow marked her mother's house:

When my mother was in charge of the kitchen house, the hoboes would come to the back door, as they did throughout the Amanas. She would always feed them, and not even make them work. She said, I know he has a mother somewhere, and she must be worried about him so I'll look after him. They would always work though. When she was no longer in the kitchen they would come to the house and do work for her there. I remember one day there were five of them, and they set about cleaning the house from top to bottom, even taking out the water pipes and polishing them.

One young man passing through even stayed with us for a while and took care of me when she was out. I remember one day later on a hobo came shuffling around to the back door, and I went out. Since it was raining I invited him in. I thought he looked familiar. I fixed him something, then when he was on his way out I said, "Frank, is that you?" He just looked at me and then left quickly, so I knew it was him, the man who had taken care of me. He was so ashamed.

Some hoboes who stayed for a while would be housed in small frame buildings on each village's borders: "hobo hotels" these houses were called.[5]

Even more exciting visitors might make their way through the Amanas. One woman was only seven years old when the most renowned of them all came to call:

My mother and my grandmother were working in the communal gardens one day when we still lived in West, and that day Jesse James and another man came. They spent the whole day sitting under a tree by the garden and talking to them. That night they robbed the store. One shot was fired by the night watchman, but nobody was hurt. Then they went on and robbed the store in South. My mother, when she learned who they were, said, "Imagine we spent the whole day talking to Jesse James."[6]

Besides such visits, the holidays provided the major changes in routine. Lasting several days, they marked a definite break, an occasion for celebrating and for much visiting. Says one now-elderly man:

The holidays were great. You know we had two days on holidays each at Christmas and New Year's. At Christmas the front room was closed and we could not go in there until Santa Claus and Kris Kringle, his wife, came to let us in. Santa Claus wore a fur coat, a mask, and one of those tall pointed hats rimmed with fur. Kris Kringle wore a white bride's dress with a veil so that you couldn't see who it was. Imagine Santa Claus coming directly to your house every year. Talk about believing.

And another woman in South Amana adds:

At Christmas the major activity would be visiting. Mother would usually bake something with ingredients she got from the kitchen and open a jar of canned preserves from her own private garden. I think we enjoyed the visiting because it was a holiday from work and school, and because we knew all the people—they were all relatives and friends—and because we got to play together with their children.

Then at Easter we again got two days off. Saturday morning, when we'd still be at school, the kitchen girls would bake the Easter rabbits—big ones—maybe ten inches long, and dye the Easter eggs. Then they would hide them around the kitchen grounds, in the garden or, if it was raining, in the woodshed. After school all the children would race home for their Easter baskets, and then all the children who were fed out of a kitchen would gather there and scatter off to look for the hidden nests. Each nest contained two Easter rabbits and six colored eggs, so that was a real treat. Mother would bake some more rabbits for us of her own.

Occasionally there would occur an event of such scale and excitement that it entered the oral history of the community. One such event linking the outside with the commune in a peculiar way was the wreck of the Rocky Mountain Limited on 21 March 1905, two miles west of Homestead.

The Rocky Mountain Limited, a crack express train of the Rock Island Railroad, was derailed while travelling about 55 miles per hour. The engine, mail car, baggage car and two sleepers went down the steep embankment with the chair car off the rails. There were fifty-three passengers on board, but only one was killed outright. The engineer was scalded and bruised so badly that he died as a result. Examination of the track showed that spikes had been pulled from the rails and bolts had been taken out of the angle bars.

The railroad had detectives on the job the next morning, and they soon found that tools were missing from the tool house of the Milwaukee railroad at Amana. Several persons knew Erich von Kutzleben had been a railroader and the character of the work showed it to be that of an experienced railroad man, so he was arrested on suspicion. He later confessed the crime. After taking the nuts off the bolts and pulling the spikes, he threw the crowbar and wrench into the water at Brush Run near the bridge. He then went about 100 feet into the timber to watch the wreck. After it had happened, he went over to it, saw the fireman, the derailed cars, and stayed in the area for about two hours. He stated that he then started to Amana about 2:30 a.m., and got to bed about 4 a.m. His desire to see a train wreck was given to the detectives as his motive.[7]

Besides outlaws, hoboes, Indians, and train wrecks, quiet Amana life would periodically be disrupted by outbreaks of major diseases or by violent accidents. One woman related her very near escape:

I was telling you about my childhood tragedies. I had several illnesses—the first was a serious bout with rheumatic fever. You know how they made ice blocks on the river? One winter day after school we all hitched a ride home on the ice truck—that was understood and fine. We were supposed to ride on the seats, but there weren't enough seats so I sat on the block of ice. Of course I came down with a fever right away, and the doctor asked me what I'd been doing. When I came to the bit about the block of ice, he said, "That's enough."

He had three very serious patients then. . . . He said every morning he woke up and thanked God that all three apparently had made it through the night.

Another woman from the same village had her own story:

Oh yes, the whooping cough, that wasn't funny. Everybody got it. When I had it bad I was twenty-one and it was summer. I had a high fever and wanted Mother to stay with me, but she went off to work in the kitchens. It was summer, as I said, and she was afraid that if she stayed home people would say it was because she didn't want to work, because she was lazy. But I was really sick with the fever, the delusions I had, it wasn't fun. Those who didn't have it so bad still went to work. It was during the harvest, with all the onions and all the dust, that was something terrible.

Such outbreaks of disease were major news, news that community leaders could shape to support their religious myth, as in the following report taken from the *Inspirations-Historie* of 1907:

The influenza, which first appeared in South Amana in the early part of January, also later spread to a greater or lesser degree to other communities, though not so severely, and until now only a few severe cases have occurred. Outside, especially in large cities, the death rates were large from influenza and also from severe contagious diseases and illnesses, such as scarlet fever, diphtheria, etc. Also, there is an epidemic of eye infection in the area, from which many in our community also suffer. So we, too, for the sake of our sins share misery, punishment, and affliction, which spread over the earth, though with much patience the Lord has sustained us and preserved our lives and spared and protected us from many severe illnesses and sacrifices, which many in the cities and areas around us endured.

On most matters the young member would have an excellent knowledge of what was expected of him or her. Work expectations were well established—indeed, not radically different from those held by the group's German forebears. Social behavior was also prescribed and enforced by a church that served as the major means of social control. On one matter, however, the young member might feel some confusion. For included among Gruber's original rules was the admonition "Fly from the society of women . . . as a very highly dangerous magnet and magical fire." Some apparently took that advice, for Amana did have a somewhat higher percentage of single people throughout the late 1800s and into the early 1900s than did the rest of the United States.[8] Others, however, apparently felt no such compunction and readily joined in the fun.

COURTSHIP AND MARRIAGE

Although the separation of the sexes at work and in church did make encounters difficult, the villages were small and the social life of adolescents and young adults was based on long-term acquaintance. Having grown up together, the young people knew each other well and had plenty of information by which to make their choices. Day's work done, they would gather in front of the village store for talk or flirtation. In the winter when the millrace froze over, skating was a major courtship activity. In the afternoon the boys would test the ice to see if it were solid and slick enough, then would stop off at the kitchen to tell the girls. In the evening they would all gather and, when everyone who was expected was there, would go down to the river.

As everywhere, attractions developed and courtships were begun. Yet carrying out the decision to marry was not easy for a young couple. First of all, marriage was not allowed until the woman was twenty and the man twenty-four, and even then the match had to win the approval of the Council of Trustees. Approval granted, the couple had to go through a one- to two-year engagement during which they lived in different villages. If the couple passed this test and could still muster some fondness for each other, the elders would pick a day for the wedding.[9]

The actual ceremony changed somewhat over the years, but it remained an occasion of great solemnity. When Nordhoff visited the colonies in 1874, the practice was to have the couple and their parents meet with the elders in the bride's home. There, as Nordhoff tells us:

After singing and prayer, the chapter of Paul's writings is read wherein, with great plainness of speech, he describes to the Ephesians and the Christian world in general the duties of husband and wife. On this chapter the elders comment "with great thoroughness" to the young people, and "for a long time," as I was told; and after this lecture, and more singing and prayer, there is a modest supper, whereupon all retire quietly to their homes.[10]

By the early 1900s the wedding had become a somewhat more festive occasion, with the modest supper becoming more and more a communal feast. When asked what she remembered of her girlhood, one woman in High Amana pointed right away to the wedding celebrations:

I remember weddings best, like Uncle Charley's wedding—that was about 1907 or 1908. All the close relatives would gather in the morning and then they have dinner and then about 1:00 they would go to church for the ceremony. They wore the regular church outfit, the black dress. The elders would perform the ceremony, which lasted an hour. No flowers, nothing like that. Then they would come home and start celebrating. They'd have plenty of food—cake, cookies, beer, crackers, and whatever you want. In the afternoon after the service those not invited to the service would all come for the celebration. In those days it was not common to go on a honeymoon. They went back to work the next day.

Divorce was not readily accepted, for the couple was assumed to have thought long and hard about their choice.

While marriage and childbearing were not exactly encouraged in Amana, the community was unusual among successful communal efforts in even allowing their presence. Kanter has demonstrated how the institution of the family can prove a major stumbling block for communal societies, and indeed the family does tend to compete with community for the loyalty of its members. Two of the most successful communities, the Shakers and Oneida, did away with the nuclear family, though what they offered in its stead represented opposite extremes, with the Shakers practicing celibacy and the Oneida adherents a form of group marriage.[11] In Amana the family remained strong, and it did present one source of contention and division as the years progressed. To compound the problem, many families had ties to relatives on the outside, either in America or in Europe, and visits and letters, while frowned upon by the authorities, were not strictly forbidden. One communard, for example, received the following letter, presumably one of many (as the letter itself indicates), from a nephew, a fairly accomplished sculptor living in Paris:

1881

My dear Uncle,

I'm counting on your very great generosity to forgive the lateness of my reply. But I wanted to give you the photo of your nephew whom you saw so small when I would call you "cake-uncle," a surname that I know as well-suited to you because both my memory and my father's word confirm it.

However that may be, when very young I recall perfectly well you saw me at the house on the rue des Prouvaires. It was I believe at the time of the departure or arrival of the troops from Italy. I was sick and consequently in bed—and it was you who helped me see the paper soldiers in the street.

As you yourself put it, that was a long time ago because I'm now 30 and the nephew of yesterday is not the same one today.[12]

The nephew then speaks of other relatives, concludes with best wishes for the new year, and promises to send the photograph in the next letter.

Such relatives on the outside not only provided a different look at the greater world and interpretations that differed from those provided by the Amana leadership, they were often also the source of prized possessions, of gifts that created distinctions among the communards. While such ties served to chip away at communal identification, the decision to allow the family to continue as an institution did mean that Amana never had to battle the "special affections"—of one man for one woman, of parents for their children—that were the bane of the Oneida society.[13]

To counter the pull of the family, the church found ways to demonstrate that celibacy was indeed the preferred state. Newlyweds would be demoted in church seating for a time, and so too would both man and woman each time the wife gave birth. Pregnant women were encouraged to conceal their condition (which, given the Amana garb, was not hard to do), and families were to be kept small, though four children were fairly common and only those families with seven or eight offspring earned the title "rabbit families."

The pull of the family was also countered by the fact that most adults spent the majority of their day in communal labor. The Inspirationists' workday started at 7:00 A.M. in summer, 7:30 A.M. in winter, and continued until supper at 6:00 P.M., broken only by dinner at noon and by midmorning and midafternoon snacks.[14] After work, evening services afforded the opportunity to reflect on the day's activities.

THE SOCIETY AND THE WORLD: PRESCRIBING AND PROSCRIBING ADULT BEHAVIOR

All these mechanisms for ensuring commitment—the emphasis on communal work and sharing, the sacrifice of individual distinction (and goods), the promise of transcendence through obedience to tradition and inspired word—were not, however, sufficient to control the will of some individuals and some families, and so stricter sanctions also came into play. These sanctions operated largely through the church, that is, through the authority of *Werkzeug* and trustees. Most of the *Werkzeuge* testimonies include admonitions and exhortations to better behavior. The trustees also could single out members, chiding them for such practices as selling fruits and vegetables for private gain or for exhibiting "vanity in dress." Absenteeism from church was another growing problem. Members might not attend services when they disagreed with an elder, and through the decades the younger adults found more and more reasons to avoid the Saturday evening service.[15]

The greatest problem the community faced was drinking. As early as 1856 Metz wrote a letter from Amana back to Ebenezer criticizing the abuse of liquor, and the community record (the *Inspirations-Historie*) notes in 1893 that "the worst of it is that a great many, and even some of the elders, do not believe that this desire for drinking is so enormous. Those who drink so much cannot work." In a society based on communal labor, not working was the worst sin of all.[16]

In addition to these more-than-daily church services, two special occasions figured large in the community's spiritual life. The *Unterredung*, a spiritual examination held once a year, was an occasion of great seriousness and was somewhat feared. Each member, down through the children, had to appear before the elders and the *Werkzeug* to confess the sins of the past year. Persons or groups who did not appear sufficiently contrite would be sent home to return the next day. The elders themselves would start the process by being examined by the elders of another village. The largest role in the ceremony, however, fell to the *Werkzeug*. The *Unterredung*, which lasted approximately a week in each village, was occasion for display of the *Werkzeug*'s charismatic authority, for at this time he or she was particularly likely to admonish erring members through inspiration. In this way the leadership effected a balance between the daily, temporal decisions made by trustees and elders and the charismatic religious authority of the *Werkzeug* that could be called on periodically to renew and reinspire the community members. The *Unterredung* was a grueling process for all. Even the youngest church members, boys and girls of seven and eight, would have to memorize at least a simple phrase: "I was bad; I will be good." Year after year more repentance would be expected, their souls and deeds more scrupulously inspected.

The other major religious occasion, the *Liebesmahl* (Lord's Supper), was far more joyous, though it too maintained a serious tone. Usually following the *Unterredung*, it was held only once every two years. It also was a time for the *Werkzeug* to play a particularly prominent role, for on this occasion the Lord was believed particularly likely to be present. All residents would gather at the church in Main Amana in their different age groups for a special service, and afterward they would be assigned to the various kitchen houses for a simple meal. It was a time for solemnity, for rejoicing, for reaffirming the solidarity of the group and its devotion to God.[17]

Thus the church operated throughout the individual member's life as a powerful system of social control. Yet there were other means available to the Amana leadership, including their considerable control over the flow of information into the colonies and their ability to interpret events in a manner consonant with the religious ideology. The *Werkzeuge* and ranking elders had always, since the early German period, maintained some links with the outside through economic ties and legal arrangements. But these leaders wisely sought to forbid the forging of similar links by the broader membership. Language, of course, worked in their favor, for until shortly before World War I many members felt uncomfortable using their limited English. Language, and with it culture, served to segregate community from outside world. While residents made and still make much of the differences among themselves (as between those of German or Swiss ancestry), when compared with the human variety found in the outside society the colonists look remarkably homogeneous. Indeed, the community was fortunate in its relative homogeneity, for attempting to weld many different peoples into a cohesive community has proved the downfall of many a communal group. Nordhoff, writing in 1879, considered a major reason for Amana's success to be its members' nationality and class background, for he believed their peasant and craftsman heritage made them more easily satisfied than many other Americans would be with the secure if sometimes boring life Amana provided. This led him to philosophize:

It seems to me that these advantages are dearer to the Germans than to almost any other nation and hence they work more harmoniously in communistic experiments. I think I noticed at Amana, and elsewhere among the German communistic societies, a satisfaction with their lives, a pride in equality which the communal system secures, and also in the conscious surrender of the individual to the general good.[18]

The relative homogeneity was certainly no accident. Since the migration to the United States, the society leadership had shrewdly limited the admission of new members. Most of those admitted came from Germany, including a large influx of new members from Saxony in 1880–82. To prove the sincerity of their intent and their ability to mold themselves to the Amana way of life, new members would undergo a two-year probation, after which they would finally be accepted as new members. Another measure of their commitment was giving up their money and possessions to the community's coffers. Such means as the careful selection, the surrender of goods, and the long probationary period effectively tested the dedication of the prospective member.[19]

The elders did not stop there. Throughout the member's life, whether he or she was among the few who joined following the migration or—more likely—was born into the society, the trustees would repeatedly interpret the outside world, easing political and natural events into the official world-view. One of the means available to them was the institution of the elders' comments at church services. Another was the yearly volumes of the *Inspirations-Historie*, the official community history. Before the 1890s very few outside events were even mentioned: those appearing in the record after that date were usually either natural or man-made disasters, as the following chronology indicates:

1892   Widespread illness, sickness all over the world,
       famine and death, especially in Russia

Cholera in Europe
Columbus Day and the World's Fair in Chicago
1893 Terrible cyclone in northwest Iowa
Fire at the World's Fair in Chicago
End of the World's Fair
1895 Tornadoes in Kansas, Iowa, and South Dakota; two cyclones in Kansas
1897 Mississippi floods its banks
1898 Outbreak of war between the United States and Spain
1900 Hurricane and flood at Galveston, Texas
1901 Day of sorrow for the murdered President William McKinley
1902 Report on the disaster on the island of Martinique
1905 Peace Congress between Russia and Japan
1906 Earthquake in San Francisco
Earthquake in Jamaica

Besides the human interest aroused by suffering and the farmer's natural obsession with the weather, natural events were of interest to the Amana leaders as examples of God's way with sinful men. On the occasion of the San Francisco earthquake (to whose victims colonists sent a railroad car full of food and merchandise), the *Inspirations-Historie* made the following comment:

So the judgments and visitations of God increase and mount to the assured race of man. However, how many take notice, mend their ways, turn to God and give him honor? The city was reputed—ahead of several other large cities—a regular cesspool. Now many thousands, especially those in the middle class, have lost everything; they are affected most severely, and many among them must have had second thoughts. But a large part of them say, "We want to rebuild this city to be more beautiful and grander than it was before," and so the impression will soon be lost again.

Thus American society was used during this period by the Amana leaders as a negative example, much as it still is today by groups such as the Amish, who point to outside disorganization (drugs, crime, and other forms of deviance) to defend their own way of life. In the *Inspirations-Historie* outsiders are repeatedly punished for their sins, but insiders, though considered spiritually superior, are also kept on their toes by an angry and jealous God. Reporting an influenza outbreak both outside and

within the Amanas, the 1906 *Inspirations-Historie* commented,
"So we too for the sake of our sins share the misery, punishment,
and affliction that spread over the earth, though, and with much
patience, the Lord has sustained us and preserved our lives and
spared and protected us from many severe illnesses and sacrifices which many in the cities and areas around us endured."
Also published in each yearbook were brief biographies of those
members who had died during the preceding year. This afforded
trustees the clear chance to pass judgment on past and, by im-
plication, present members. Indeed, both behavioral norm and
deviation from it may best be seen by contrasting the biographies
of two community members. The first, one Sister Theresa: [20]

. . . was born in Baierthal, Baden, one of the daughters of Br. Jacob—
who died in Ober Ebenezer in the distressed year 1850. At the time of
the emigration she came with her mother and sister to Amana. In her
youth she became engaged to a young man . . . the engagement, however, was terminated by his death, so she remained single and in the
years to come became a faithful and devout Sister and the internal
support of her family and relatives, especially since the death of her
mother. . . .

In her younger years she was healthy and active, but later on ailing
and sickly and could no longer do heavy work, but busied herself with
light handwork and sewing. She remained steadfast and industrious in
whatever she could still do. She had a good understanding of the spiritual, acquired through the school of suffering and disappointments experienced by herself and the next of kin, which taught her faith and
prayer. For almost a year now, more or less, she has been consumptive,
often confined and often with great shortness of breath; in the last few
weeks especially she had to endure a painful ordeal. But she was calm
and patient and resigned to the will of God until finally the bitter cup of
death was drunk and emptied her soul, through the help and grace of
her savior and redeemer Jesus Christ, passed through death and into the
true life.

Contrast such praise and assurances of heavenly reward to the
official opinion on another departed:

. . . Brother Eberhard, though ailing, was the night before still cheerful
and reading his paper but was found dead in his room in the morning.
He was single, born in Cologne and arrived in the Ebenezer community
in the year 1860, after he had been with a Shaker community. However,

in July 1862 he left the community and joined a military unit in Buffalo. At the end of the war, during the summer of 1865, he came to Amana and asked for readmission into the community, which was granted him.

But his future life did not take a good course. He was given to heavy drinking, sought and found despite all warning the means and ways to indulge. He began to suffer physically from rheumatism, which he attributed to battle fatigue suffered during the war. Since the United States government for a number of years now had been granting an increased pension and back pay for all who were injured during the war, he handed in an application for a pension and received it, which came to quite a sum and which he continued to receive monthly. This money, however, was his total downfall, yes, the ruination of body and soul. More and more he gave in to his passion, whereby he became progressively weaker and more disabled and therefore often needed assistance. . . . The elders often urgently protested to him concerning his disorderly life and his squandering of money and how he was doing himself the greatest harm thereby. It was all to no avail, and so it was in such circumstances a genuine burden and worry to the elders how things might turn out with him. So now, suddenly, the end has come.

Yet even this member, recalcitrant and disapproved of to the last, had been able to enjoy one of the great advantages of Amana life—the respect in which most elderly were held and the ways they continued to be integrated into community and family life. By all reports, people tended to live longer in the old Amana than on the outside and could stay active longer, working at least part time.[21] Elderly members often lived next door to or in the same house with their grown children, yet their separate apartments afforded them privacy when they wanted it. Most had also developed skill at some craft—knitting, whittling, or such—that could be carried on and admired. They also had the function of telling stories to their grandchildren, stories that often spoke of the voyage from Germany to New York and then to Iowa, sagas of the difficult early years, or tales of the inspiration of Christian Metz.[22]

As oral historian Ronald Blythe has written, "It is the nature of old men and women to become their own confessors, poets, philosophers, apologists, and storytellers."[23] Given free rein, Amana residents who remember the old days would paint an even rosier picture than the one presented here. But when their accounts are coupled with documents from the period and placed in the historical setting of Iowa County history, they tell of a social life based on family and village where work was hard, visits even to the other Amana villages rare, and a daily routine at once comforting and wearing, broken only by an occasional visit by an outsider, by illness or accident, or by holidays or wedding celebrations. Soon, however, new sources of excitement would be added that would draw the colonists not only out of their daily routines but out of their distinctive way of life.

PART II

Economic Transformations

CHAPTER 5

$\mathbb{A}$ LETTER delivered to the Homestead broom maker in 1932 was one small result of the transformations the Amana economy experienced between the 1870s and the 1890s.

Mr. Carl Hess, broom maker
Homestead, Iowa   April 1932

Dear Mr. Hess:
    Please be advised that the new system will go into effect next Monday morning, May 2nd.
    Also please take notice that your shop is to be closed, at least for the time being.
    Later on we will give further consideration as to the matter of shops and then either continue to operate them by the society, sell or rent to the individual, or close some of them permanently.

    Yours truly,
    Arthur Barlow
    Business Manager[1]

The numerous cabinetmaking shops, tin shops, shoemaker, watch-repair, harness, and blacksmith shops, and many others added up to more than fifty small enterprises, all operating under the communal rubric. Nobody worried much about the system's efficiency, for the shops existed to serve the villagers instead of some abstract principle. As long as the colonies prospered, which they did, such small shops seemed a rational part of the village-based economy and social structure.

But what appears rational in one time may be ill adapted to a later time. This village-based organization of the Amanas was appropriate to the period in America's history when local community was the focus of life and the basis for most economic exchange. The low productivity associated with Amana's decentralized and small-scale operation, combined with the high waste reported in the distribution of goods from communal kitchens and the large number of outsiders hired to do the work of malingering communards, grew into a major problem as this village-based economy became increasingly anachronistic and as America became a national society and economy.

THE NATIONAL PICTURE

In the late 1800s and early 1900s the United States was becoming fused by a national transportation and communications network. This network was creating a national economy in which the Amana mills were placed in competition with large eastern woolen mills and also were exposed to the fluctuating demands of a national economy moving through war into peace. Agricultural production became rationalized as it grew in scale, and farm areas like the Amanas became linked to the growing urban centers. New values accompanied the changing structure as a new myth emerged out of the interpretation of "modern" life. Indeed, in considering the response to industrialization during 1885–1914, historian Samuel Hays believes that the social changes during this period were greater than ever before in American history. Speaking of how one hypothetical citizen might have experienced this transformation, Hays writes, "Had he been a manufacturer, a merchant, a laborer, or a farmer, the American of 1914 would have experienced the transition from relatively stable, local business affairs to intense nationwide competition that rendered his way of living far less secure."[2] He would have seen new transportation lines linking every group into "one interdependent nation." He would have experienced the advent of a new factory-based method of production requiring large amounts of capital and new technology. He would have been witness to the subordination of religion, education, and politics to the one goal of creating wealth, to the extent that "increasing production, employment and income became the measures of community success, and personal riches the mark of individual achievement."[3]

While stressing in particular the rise of the bureaucratic order out of this economic transition, historian Robert Wiebe agrees with Hays on the magnitude of the changes involved. Characterizing nineteenth-century America as "a society of island communities,"[4] he writes: "The heart of American democracy was local autonomy. A century after France had developed a reasonably efficient, centralized public administration, Americans could not even conceive of a managerial government. Almost all of a community's affairs were still arranged informally."[5]

Both historians see the autonomy of the local community as being eroded by a number of forces. The extension of the railroad throughout the West and Midwest during the second half of the 1800s both spurred production, indirectly encouraging the development of new techniques of mass production, and offered previously unavailable goods for consumption in far-flung communities. Advances in communications—the telegraph, and later the telephone, the modern press, and nationwide advertising— joined with improved transportation to create a national economy. Other major changes included a shift from largely subsistence farming to commercial farming. Whereas an old-style farmer relied on traditional methods and wisdom to make a living from his small stake, the new farmer believed in capital investment and fancy equipment, more scientific training, and attention to market fluctuations. By the turn of the century the farmer was "irrevocably entwined in the complex industrial system. Not as a Jack-of-all-trades, but only as a calculating, alert, and informed businessman could he survive.[6]

ON THE FARM

Iowa reflected these national changes, and in the late 1860s and 1870s Iowa farmers already found themselves threatened. The railroads in particular were seen as abusing the farmers by charging more for short hauls than for long ones and by giving preferential treatment to large shippers. Next to the railroads the farmers distrusted the middlemen, who in marketing the farmers' produce were seen as pocketing most of the profits. Partly in response to these tensions and partly to educate the farmer and his family in the new agricultural methods, the Grange arose as an important rural institution. The first Iowa chapter was founded in 1868 in Newton, and the Grange achieved tremendous popularity throughout the state, for all the reasons above and also because it provided a social life and an improved sense of status for farm families. By Grange standards, at least, they were not to be considered inferior to city-dwellers but instead were "producers" as opposed to "nonproducers." The Grange was successful in getting legislation to regulate the railroads (though this legislation had to be amended to produce the desired effect) and in marketing farm produce cooperatively. It was dramatically unsuccessful in its attempt to produce farm equipment, misjudging its market completely, a critical mistake that led to its decline in importance and power during the late 1870s.[7]

In contrast to this early enthusiastic response to the Grange as an organization speaking for the farmer, Iowa farmers were less enthusiastic about backing the Populist movement. The state as a whole failed to vote for William Jennings Bryan in the critical 1896 presidential election. While the reasons for this lukewarm response were several, the cardinal one was that Iowa did not appear as poorly off in the 1890s as did Kansas, Nebraska, or North and South Dakota, major sources of Populist support:

While Iowa had its troubles, what with low prices for farm produce, heavy mortgage indebtedness at exorbitant rates of interest . . . , high freight rates, and adverse weather conditions, such factors were not as severely felt in Iowa as in the [other states mentioned]. A high percentage of the mortgages were of the constructive and investment type, farm tenancy was not the result of a land monopoly in the hands of nonresident owners, and the restriction of the railroads under the new laws of 1878, 1884, and 1888 afforded some relief. The east central counties . . . were developing a new and more profitable type of agriculture which utilized Iowa's grain and hay for hog- and cattle-feeding operations, and the northeast counties added large-scale dairying, thus relieving the dependence on railroads and producing more cash income.[8]

Although in the 1880s Iowa was still predominantly a farming
state, by 1880 it had already reached its maximum rural population. From that date forward the urban areas grew at the expense
of the rural areas. As of 1880 Des Moines, the largest city, had a
population of only 22,408, but this reached 50,093 in 1890 and
62,139 in 1900. By 1880 the major period of the state's settlement was clearly over: the growth rate for the decade 1870–80
was only 76 percent as contrasted to 251.1 percent for the previous decade and 345.8 for the decade before that. In the decade
1900–1910 the state actually lost population, since rural residents not attracted to the cities or not finding jobs in industry left
the state, some drawn by cheaper land prices elsewhere in the
West and Midwest.[9]

After 1900, however, the lot of the farmer temporarily improved. American farmers were entering what has been termed
"the golden age of agriculture," when American farm produce
reached out toward a broader world market. Farmers benefited
further when America entered World War I, and demand for produce overseas, assisted by government support and regulation of
pricing, encouraged many farmers to mortgage their farms to acquire more land. "Food will win the war," was the slogan, and the
patriotic thing to do was to plant more, grow more, ship more.[10]

It did not take much imagination to see that the war's end
would mean massive surpluses and a disastrous fall in prices.
Henry C. Wallace, later named secretary of agriculture under
Harding, did foresee the problem and warned that the farmer
should be taken back down the ladder rung by rung.[11] But his
advice was not heeded. With the war's end, the guaranteed price
on wheat was abruptly withdrawn and so, too soon, were government supports for other crops. The farmers who had been advised to assume heavy mortgages to buy more land now, in a time
of contracting markets, saw those mortgages come due, and
many could not make the payments or prevent foreclosure. Rural
recession thus accompanied the urban prosperity of the 1920s.
Whereas in 1919 farmers held 16 percent of the national income,
by 1929 the figure had declined to 9 percent.[12] The sense of deprivation was made all the more severe by the new emphasis on
consumerism, with new goods entering the market, advertising

expanding, and buying on credit becoming an acceptable practice. The farmer's family, struggling to make ends meet, looked with envy upon the urban wealth in which they were apparently not to share.[13] In a few years' time their discontent would spill over into a radicalism that surprised many who little realized what was happening on the farm in the age of prosperity.

Although Amana was subject to these major political and economic trends, it is possible that the colonies, composing as they did the "largest farm in Iowa," could well have benefited from the new economies of scale in a way not open to the small Iowa farmer. Certainly the Hutterites living on the Great Plains had managed not only to achieve benefits of scale through large acreages, accumulated capital, and ready labor, but to add willingness to experiment with new equipment and new farming methods. Many localities that had opposed the Hutterites during World War I because of their German language and their pacifism now welcomed them as they brought the cash to buy mortgaged land and pay local taxes.[14] Amana's failure to adopt similar strategies, its sticking to the old German village-based system, may have contributed to its major economic difficulties and decline as a communal sect. Significantly, one of the community's first moves in the 1932 reorganization was to hire an outside businessman and efficiency expert, who immediately set about modernizing the Amana economy by closing down unprofitable craft shops such as Mr. Hess's broom shop and creating order out of a thoroughly chaotic bookkeeping system. But other factors were at least as important as the village structure per se, ranging from the difficulties of keeping members' store spending in line to the rising cost of hired help to the condition of the woolen mill after 1924. Let us trace some of the steps that led to the economic decline so that we may better understand the decision that was in time faced and made by the community.

WITHIN THE AMANAS

The major difficulties arose because the Amanas had never achieved economic independence from the larger society and because after the turn of the century they were increasingly tied to the national market, especially through their woolens manufacture. In the early twentieth century small mills throughout the Midwest were threatened by shrinking markets and growing competition from the larger eastern mills. Within Amana the farm departments, the stores, and the woolen mills show the greatest variation in profits in the pre-Change years, exactly those sections of economy that were most strongly related to the national economy through fluctuations in the availability of raw materials, in weather-affected farm prices, and in the pricing of farm products and finished woolens. The most stable institutions of the colony's economy were the village craft shops, more oriented toward internal colony needs.[15]

The growing influence of the outside society on the Amana economy is reflected in the community ledger. Andelson reports that from 1901 through 1915 good years alternated with bad, with a net loss of $15,000 for the period. The decline may actually be traced to the years following 1881, when the community's net worth was $1,347,669, its highest until 1918. While Andelson admits that assessing the Society's economic state throughout these years is difficult, he does conclude that profits were uncertain at best—that the trend was "generally up" from 1885 until 1900 and "generally down" thereafter.[16]

This downward trend was halted by the outbreak of World War I and the awarding of an armed services contract to the woolen mills. Prosperity continued throughout the war years and up through 1922. Andelson writes:

In 1922 the Society presented an economically sound picture. Its net profit that year was $6,700. The woolen mills were the largest credit department, with profits of $80,000. The capital account was the largest in Amana history, $1,216,000. The Society's net worth, $1,697,000, was also the highest ever. If the Society's capital and net worth had been distributed equally among its members in 1922, each person would have received $2,000 compared to $1,375 in 1901. Total profits from 1901 to 1922 were $180,000, compared to losses of $91,000.[17]

The next year, however, the bottom fell out of the woolen market owing to the termination of the army contracts. Whereas in 1922 the woolens profit was $80,000, in 1923 it was down to $36,000, less than half. Feed mill profits also fell $7,000; grain and lumber profits dropped $3,000 in 1923, $4,000 the following year. Meanwhile taxes had increased $3,000 in 1923 and $4,000 the next year. Andelson comments that these factors combined to make 1923 "the worst year financially in Amana history." From that year on the final annual economic report would be in the red.[18]

While profits fluctuated widely for these years, costs grew steadily. Whereas "from 1901 to 1918 Amana's cost account averaged $30,000 annually, thereafter it rose to an average of $42,000."[19] Along with national inflation and higher taxes, another cost was created by hired hands from the outside. Brought in first to help during the Iowa construction period, in 1863 they already numbered nearly 100 when total Society membership was 1,027. By 1880 there were 200, more than one-tenth of the total population, and there were still approximately that many in 1932. Housed on the borders of each village in the "hobo hotels," they worked primarily at the unskilled jobs on the farms and in the mills. Their cost to the community was approximately $28,000 a year, a cost many felt would be unnecessary if the colonists themselves could be inspired to work harder. But with the increasing defection of younger members and increased national inflation, the Society was forced to pay its hands ever-higher wages in the postwar period.[20]

One incident highlights some of the failings of the old system, in particular the leaders' lack of foresight in failing to anticipate difficulties and adapt to the new economic realities. The following headline and article appeared in the *Cedar Rapids Republican* on Sunday, 12 August, 1923.

AMANA SOCIETY SUFFERS BIG LOSS:
TEN BUILDINGS WIPED OUT BY FIRE

Flour and Woolen Mills with Power Plant
Devoured in a Few Hours.

Amid the peaceful vine-clad and flower-bedecked homes of Amana, the cry of fire resounded just as the peaceful and God-fearing folk were enjoying their noon-day meal yesterday. Within three hours an inferno of flames had destroyed the colony's two great industries, the flouring mills and the woolen mills. Ten great buildings burned with a fury before which hundreds of firefighters were powerless and the loss is conservatively estimated at $250,000. It may run much higher; some estimates place it at half a million.[21]

The Amanas carried no insurance. Nor had they ever laid away funds in times of prosperity. Coupled with the failing market for woolens, increasing costs, and competition, this fire and its revelation of the community leaders' lack of foresight spelled economic doom for the communal structure.

Given the leaders' proclivity for seeing disasters as God's punishing a wayward people, this fire might have been interpreted as a call to renewed faith. But the communalism myth, with its structure, had been suffering its own reverses. In 1906, for example, when the market for woolens was booming and the Amanas were falling far behind on their orders, it was decided to take on overtime workers at the woolen mills. Previously, anytime extra hands were needed they would be drafted from wherever they could be spared within the colony: if the wagon shop could spare a man, or if fewer men could make do in the fields, recruits would be sent to help out as needed. By 1906, however, this spirit of cooperation seemed to be lacking. For the first time ever, these workers demanded and received overtime pay. This action opened a Pandora's box of personal demands. Soon others were demanding and getting extra pay for milking cows in addition to their regular jobs. Moonlighting agricultural workers earned two or two and a half cents a bushel, and anyone who worked in any shop, such as the harness, blacksmith, or carpentry shops, was now unofficially allowed to stay on after the regular hours to do his own work, accepting orders from the outside.

Indeed, the society's members were proving remarkably adept at finding ways to earn money. Hunting and trapping were popular sources of income, as was canning fruits and vegetables to sell to outsiders. Women might sell their "fancywork" and men, as above, their craftwork. The Amana skills and standards of workmanship were well respected on the outside, and many on the inside apparently found individual profit more inspiring than the motive of communal gain.

In addition, misuse of communal trust for individual gain— and lack of punishment by the authorities—became increasingly common. Andelson recounts the following instances:

Following a sale to outsiders in the later 1920's, a basketmaker went to the store intending to turn the money over to the Society, according to the rules. The clerk told him to keep the money for himself since "everyone does it." Another man returned to the Society from his training at a teacher's college with a careful account of his expenses and all the money the Society provided him and that had not been used. Impressed by the man's honesty and frugality, the elder gave him some silver dollars to keep. These and similar instances would not have happened under the stricter regime of inspiration.[22]

The sanctions that might have been applied under the stricter regime had lost much of their bite. Being placed in a lower rank or bench in church was no longer taken so seriously. The sterner punishment of being locked out of church was viewed as a holiday by some of the young. Clearly, the traditional legitimation of religious authority had been seriously undermined along with the Amana economy. Individual choices were being legitimated by a new and different myth, one stressing individualistic, bureaucratic, and rationalistic values above the values of piety and self-surrender. Along with the demands of a new economic order, however, the Inspirationist dogma was also coming under attack from a second source: the penetration of the community's boundaries by a competing religion.

Religious Revolt

CHAPTER 6

ALTHOUGH the debate over secularization is complex, it is generally agreed that toward the end of the nineteenth century and into the early twentieth century churches appeared to be losing both traditional moral authority and church members. The processes of urbanization and industrialization were indeed bringing new values and new leaders to the fore, and churches, while still playing an important symbolic role, had less power as moral arbiters.[1]

There were, of course, important countertrends. One response was the emergence of a "social gospel" movement that sought a more active role in solving the social problems of the day. A second response was to affiliate religion with the world of business, in the hope that some of the businessman's status and glamour would rub off on the churchman. The best example was the runaway success in 1925 of Bruce Barton's *The Man Nobody Knew*, which likened Jesus Christ to a crackerjack salesman. Jesus, according to Barton, "picked up twelve men from the bottom ranks of business and forged them into an organization that conquered the world."[2]

Third, while many mainstream denominations were losing members, one rather new denomination was rapidly gaining them. In the decades 1900–1910 and 1910–20 Mary Baker Eddy's Christian Science was being spread by a small army of practitioners who were trained in Boston and operated across the states. Their message, "that there is no life, truth, intelligence, nor substance in matter," appealed to many sick people whom doctors had given up on. The Christian Science doctrine, with its positive outlook, its mysticism, and its rigorous demands, appealed to a number of families within the Amanas and was therefore judged a threat to the community at large. For community was still defined as church: to question religious authority was to question the political authority of the Amana elders and trustees.[3]

Questioning of religious dogma and authority, however, did not start in the 1920s or even in the 1910s. As early as the Ebenezer period there had been cracks in the religious wall, with outside temptations affecting even that first generation of communards. What the leaders perceived as spiritual laxness continued after the move to Iowa. In an 1865 letter to a woman in South Amana, Metz complained that the people of West Amana were not devout and that as a consequence he had not had an inspiration there for two years.[4] After Metz's death in 1867 and Landmann's death in 1883 it became ever more difficult to maintain the religious dogma in the face of threats from the outside. Belief could be just as threatening as unbelief, if it was belief in a different doctrine.

One of the earliest mentions of Christian Science in the Amanas is in the 1906 volume of the *Inspirations-Historie*, where the following report was made during the board of trustees' visit to Homestead:

A warning was issued against a false teaching which tried to establish itself in the community. . . . A so-called healing practitioner of Christian Science, who was at one time a member of our Society and sought to insinuate himself for the purpose of practicing his method of healing, was excluded. This sect professes to cure illnesses and infirmities through prayer and apparently bases its healing methods on Scripture and the power to heal the sick which Jesus gave his followers, the apostles. However, life and conduct show it is principally a moneymaking operation and that these teachings do not harmonize with the teaching of the cross and the suffering of Jesus, but it is a pharisaical and misleading conception.

Little official mention occurs after this, and members of this faith then living in the Amanas report that it went underground until 1915–20, when the elders again were forced to recognize the seriousness of its challenge. In 1916 the board of trustees chose the occasion of a member's death to lash out against all followers of Christian Science:

Brother Johannes ——— died of pneumonia at Homestead on January 7, after a short illness. He was a devoted Brother . . . and since he possessed an honest, intellectual mind, he was elevated to the position of elder in 1905. Because of trouble with his eyes he could not participate in conducting church services and prayer meetings for some years, but an improvement in this condition permitted him to resume his former duties. He lived in a kitchen house with his oldest daughter Marie, where he was a valuable aid to her. It is therefore lamentable that, in spite of his keen perception and community spirit, after a time he permitted himself to be influenced by the teachings of Christian Science, even though the Brother was often seriously and emphatically advised against it, but in the various communities, and especially in Homestead, it was accepted by many. Christian Science was introduced in the community in 1906 by a defector and found approval and entry here and there among ailing people, to whom it was presented under a good light but based on false pretenses without its anti-Christ nature being recognized. So at first many were attracted and drawn in in good faith, in the belief that they would be healed. The great evil is that through their reading of the books they disavowed the sacredness of Jesus, discarding his ministry. . . . They glorify and praise him but deny his sacredness and discard him as our Savior, also they do not heed the knowledge of the elders and their warnings. May God grant that Brother ——— did not lose his faith in our Lord and Savior, but in time attained the correct viewpoint and with remorse and repentance overcame his misunderstanding.

Contrast this stance with a discussion of an unfavorable article that appeared in the *Marengo Republican* that same year, 1916, concerning the Amana community's attitude toward Christian Science:

While the *Unterredung* was in session last week in West Amana, there appeared in the *Marengo Republican* several very hostile and slanderous articles about the community. In the first article a big exaggeration was made involving the teachings of Christian Science. It said that a discourse regarding Christian Science took place in Homestead, that its adherents rose up and a revolt and rupture threatened, which might have even as its result the splitting up of the community. The article was written in a big misunderstanding of the circumstances and false representation of the facts . . . all out of impatience with those of a different mind and belief, all based on a false and hateful sense. No particular importance should be attached to the article because the man's work treats its subject deceptively and only the false judgment of uninformed masses surrenders to it.

In the next issue of the paper followed another article full of gross untruths and distortions. . . . In it the board of trustees was blamed for unfairly enticing and forcing the adherents to disavow Christian Science. The board was investing a large amount of capital for its own account, as well as with the suppression and slavish treatment of their members. The elders themselves were said to always take advantage and enrich themselves at the cost of the subordinate members. The article lied well and extravagantly . . . and especially tried to justify the incursion of suspicion, discord, and unhappiness and to present the community to the world in an unfavorable light and thus awaken animosity against it.

Other newspapers also published commentaries, even though the articles stemmed mostly from envy and jealousy against the community and from instigation by unfriendly forces inside and outside the community and were written by an inexperienced and unqualified young reporter of the newspaper (who must be held accountable and retract the fallacious reports). To accomplish this retraction, two elders drove to Marengo on Saturday afternoon and held a meeting with the publisher of the newspaper in the presence of the community lawyer. The publisher was told of the great injustice of the false reports, the slander, and the harm and aftereffects on the good name and reputation the community had earned for itself on the outside and in the business world. It was demanded that he recall the articles and he was handed a refutation wherein the innocence of the statements was asserted, the false and slanderous statements were denied. At first he acted very pompous and arrogant, standing on his position as a newspaperman to draw news from various sources in and outside the community. But he finally understood that his arguments were baseless. The refutation was published in his newspaper, not word for word, but in substance. Since he is without means, unfortunately, no suit can be instituted against him.

Here the official report, never missing a chance to moralize and draw out a lesson for the community, went on to comment:

The contents of the articles gave evidence that the major motivation behind them was envy and jealousy, in that they sought to show that the outside world, and especially Marengo, had nothing to gain from the community. Yet it has to be regarded as an admission by the Lord that much has gone on in the community that is neither good nor praiseworthy, especially through the many sins and mingling with the outside world and the defectors. This has vexed the Master so that the evil one and his instruments received the power to spread over the community and to oppress it. This caused the elders and the sincere a great deal of grief and concern, as many neighbors and business friends seized upon these rudely slanderous accusations. May God not withdraw from us his guidance and protection, but turn back all the powers of evil, both from within and without, and bring them to naught.[5]

Amana people involved with Christian Science during this period stress its inherent difficulties and the discipline demanded in following this particular creed. Besides potential healing, Christian Science may have offered some residents an alternative to the collapsing Inspirationist dogma, though they themselves may have perceived the new religion as a "supplement" to the community faith. One religious sect is here invaded by another whose service and structure bear a curious resemblance to those of the first. The doctrine of both sects was provided by an "inspired" leader; both emphasize self-denial, strict division between good and evil, and the necessity of proving faith through everyday activities. In addition, the conduct of Christian Science services bears some resemblance to the Amana services. Though readers take the place of elders, there is an emphasis on simplicity in church decor and in worship, and on certain occasions members are called on to account for the role of their religion in their lives (Wednesday-night testimonial meetings for Scientists, the *Unterredung* for Inspirationists). Such similarities are not wholly accidental, since Mary Baker Eddy was influenced somewhat by the theology and practice of the Shakers, in particular by the figure of Mother Ann. Mrs. Eddy was herself called "Mother" by her followers, and the church in Boston is considered the mother church. It has been suggested—and the sex ratios appear to bear it out—that her church was particularly appealing to women, because of her own leadership and because of the gentleness of her message.[6]

It is nonetheless difficult to be precise about how many turned to Christian Science during these early days: such behavior was, after all, clandestine and disapproved of. The total number of families involved may not have exceeded ten. It also appears however, that the families more or less secretly following Christian Science were disproportionately located in West Amana, South Amana, and Homestead, the villages with the easiest access to the outside (Homestead and South Amana through the railroad, West Amana through its proximity to Marengo). But a few families in such "interior" villages as High and Middle Amana also followed the teachings. The identification of participants was very much by family. It usually started when someone fell seriously ill and other family members had connections, either in the village itself or in another village, to someone who practiced Christian Science and who knew one of the practitioners from Iowa City, Cedar Rapids, or Des Moines. The practitioner would visit the sick person, and if a healing was perceived most of the family would turn to Christian Science. There was much curiosity, particularly in the three villages above, about who was and who was not following this religion: gossip would start any time a practitioner came to call. Periodically the elders would use the church services to inveigh against the inroads being made by Christian Science, calling it "the devil's work" and leaving little doubt of who in the room was implicated. Further, as Andelson notes, Scientists were treated as less than full members of the community. "Often they were buried at the ends of rows in the cemetery, and no testimonials were read at their funeral services."[7]

The tension came to a head after 1924, when the board of trustees decided that members of this faith would not be allowed to attend the *Unterredung* or, by a second decree, the *Liebesmahl.*

When this [decree] was read in church, a member of the South Amana congregation who was also a follower of Christian Science stood up and said, "Christian Science is not against and does not interfere with *Liebesmahl.*" The act in itself was unique, since members did not speak in church unless directed to; the message communicated by the act, "This is a bad rule," was also virtually unique. Rarely if ever had dissatisfied members gone beyond disobedience and tried to alter a ruling of the elders, especially one concerning so sacred a matter as *Liebesmahl.*[8]

An Amana picnic

Grounds of the Museum of Amana History with the Museum building at left and the restored wash house building at right. 1980 photograph by Joan Liffring-Zug

Early threshing machines. Glass negative from the collection of Joan Liffring-Zug

An Amana Society truck at the West Amana Store, circa 1920.
From the collection of Joan Liffring-Zug

Visitors to the Amana woolen mills in early 1900s. Mill workers in foreground.
From the collection of Joan Liffring-Zug

Amana woman with garden produce, circa 1920s. Photograph by William Noe.
Courtesy Museum of Amana History

Amana women shelling seed corn, circa 1935. Photograph by William Noe.
Courtesy Museum of Amana History

Amana Flour Mills, 1910. Destroyed by fire, August 11, 1922

Amana classroom, circa 1915. From William Noe Collection,
courtesy Museum of Amana History

Interior of the Homestead Church of the Community of True Inspiration, 1966.
Photograph by Joan Liffring-Zug

Amana General Store. Courtesy of State Historical Society

Amana General Store, late 1970s. Photograph by Diane Barthel

Amana Refrigeration Plant. Photograph by Diane Barthel

This outbreak in church was reported to the trustees. As it turned out, the *Liebesmahl* was not held at all that year or ever again until 1956, some thirty years later.[9]

Some present Christian Scientists remember the trouble they faced, since Amana then was defined and controlled by the church. A woman in Middle Amana spoke of the strain that existed then—and exists to a more limited extent today—in following a doctrine different from that of her neighbors:

We first turned to Christian Science in, I guess it was, 1925. My mother-in-law was very sick. There were a lot of people reading Christian Science, but they did it secretly because the elders didn't approve. In South we would meet in a grove on top of a hill. One of the elders came squawking and saying the meetings should be banned. There were always some elders like that trying to get on the other elders. But my father-in-law, who was both an elder and a trustee, said the meetings could go on, because he felt we would continue even if we were banned. You can't stop people from reading. . . .

Now I still have a friend at the reading room in Cedar Rapids, and she says a lot of Amana people come in secretly to read or buy the *Quarterly*. They don't want to attend the church.

Others found the conflict too great and left the community. Still other residents found different means of rebellion. Some stopped attending church or attended only periodically, sometimes as an explicit response to an unfavorable elder decision. In 1924 one young physician, on the birth of his second child, refused to assume a seat in the lower-ranked congregation, saying, "Having children is human nature; it has nothing to do with religion."[10] After that incident couples with newborn children were no longer demoted in church. In 1931 an even more revealing episode occurred in which a young man who had engaged in premarital sexual intercourse did not suffer the usual punishment of expulsion from church for a year but instead was allowed both to continue attending church and to marry the young woman involved before the end of the usual one-year waiting period.[11]

Such individual and collective acts of revolt are indicative of a spreading delegitimation of religious authority throughout the Amanas in the period before 1932. With the *Werkzeuge* dead and no one emerging to take their place, with the trustees unable to call on the same divine inspiration and themselves not following to the letter the religious tenets they imposed on followers, belief in the sanctity of inspiration and the superiority of communalism faded. For some Christian Science filled the gap. But most other members participated, if unconsciously, in the trend toward secularization that was felt throughout the nation in the early 1900s. During this period many people appeared, on the surface at least, to be far less preoccupied with questions of faith and salvation and far more concerned with the excitement and promise of a growing consumer society. Amana people, like others elsewhere, were subject to the almost mystical attraction of this new consumerism that, while not a formal religion, did carry its own set of values and moral guidelines.

The Rise of Consumerism

CHAPTER 7

AMONG the many enticements luring colo-
nists out of the communal structure and into the modern world
were such varied items as birthday cards and baby carriages, motion pictures and automobiles. What these diverse items had in
common was their temptation to individual statement and personal consumption. Such goods came to symbolize modernity
and the new industrializing and urbanizing society. This growing
force of consumerism was affecting small towns throughout the
nation, destroying whatever community integrity they may have
once had and forcing them to negotiate a new relationship with
the increasingly powerful urban centers. Nowhere was this process so clearly seen as in Amana, where the boundaries between
community and outside world were so high but were broached
nonetheless.

MODERN TIMES

"Modernity" and "modernization" are awkward terms of too
many uses: they have, for example, been called upon to describe
both revolutionary and post–World War II America.[1] They once
provided the dominant framework for the study of social change
in Third World nations, but social scientists, dissatisfied with
their lack of precision and the political implications involved,
have since begun to use and develop other models. The words

also assume a different meaning in literature and the arts. Here, however, I am interested not so much in the theoretical or sociologically "correct" use of the terms as in what they actually meant to the people using them in this particular period. I am interested primarily in what were considered the fruits of modern society in the late nineteenth and early twentieth centuries.

Speaking in 1962 Iowa's Henry A. Wallace, onetime Progressive candidate for president, said, "The automobile, good roads, and electricity destroyed the United States I had come to love and understand."[2] The automobile certainly did carry a revolution in its wake, particularly in the rural areas. It helped the values of an urbanizing America to push out the values of an earlier time. Key rural institutions such as the village school and the country doctor became anachronisms as easy transportation increased centralization and improved the quality of services available.[3]

Though the earliest automobiles were gentlemen's playthings, by 1920 the automobile had become democratized so that even the common man could buy a Ford. The independence that came with the car helped sever the power of local authorities, as the young used this new form of transportation both to escape and to shop around—for everything from church services to roadside amusements. Curiously, while the automobile reinforced the American myth of noble individualism and freedom, it also fortified the image of the patriarchal family with the husband very definitely in the driver's seat. Early auto excursions assumed a "gypsying" cast as the menfolk saw to the route and to setting up camp, while women did the cooking and cleaning—somewhat lesser adventures.[4]

This pattern is not so surprising, for with modernity came reemphasis of, rather than serious questioning of, dominant sex-role patterns. Carrie Chapman Catt, a former schoolteacher from Clinton, Iowa, who led the suffragettes to their final victory in 1919–20, saw Iowa women, like so many others, as interested in voting but even more interested in whether high-school girls should be allowed to wear lipstick and bob their hair.[5] While political activism continued after suffrage, new clothes and cosmetics seemed to offer many young women a greater, if deceptive, liberation.[6]

Such developments were encouraged by two other modern institutions: the department store, emerging as a feminine home away from home, and advertising, then coming of age as a respectable and expanding profession. Many of the largest department stores had their heyday in the late 1800s and early 1900s, providing new purpose and excitement for the urban woman, an excitement that Theodore Dreiser effectively captured in his novel *Sister Carrie*. The department stores, wrote Dreiser, "were handsome, bustling, successful affairs, with a host of clerks and a swarm of patrons":

Carrie passed along the busy aisles, much affected by the remarkable displays of trinkets, dress goods, stationery, and jewelry. . . . She could not help feeling the claim of each trinket and valuable upon her personally. . . . Not only did Carrie feel the drag of desire for all that was new and pleasing in apparel for women, but she noticed too, with a touch at heart, the fine ladies who elbowed and ignored her, . . . themselves eagerly enlisted in the materials which the store contained. . . . A flame of envy lighted in her heart. She realised in a dim way how much the city held—wealth, fashion, ease—every adornment for women, and she longed for dress and beauty with a whole heart.[7]

Slightly later, in the 1920s, advertising also entered a period of great development. In 1925 it might still feel called upon to justify itself as "moral" (it was, after all, tempting people to buy), but soon thereafter it began enthusiastically introducing the American public to new and presumably desirable goods: cosmetics, electric appliances, items for personal hygiene.[8] The modern woman was told to look both to herself and to her home. Feminist proposals for cooperative experiments in housing were swept aside or purposely undermined as the spacious suburban home, reinforcing the structure of the nuclear family and the woman's place in it, became the norm—certainly a most profitable one.[9]

Still another commercial development must be added to this brew: the pictures. The role models for women in the twenties and thirties came not from the struggle for suffrage but from the silver screen, and men's heroes also changed from heroes of production (though Henry Ford and Thomas Alva Edison still attracted a following) to heroes of consumption, men such as Babe Ruth and Douglas Fairbanks.[10] Movies changed often, and people went often. Iowa writer Clarence Andrews recalls how "the often grim realities of growing up in an Iowa workingman's home . . . were made easier by the hours spent in the Palace, the Strand, the Olympia, the Rialto, the Capitol, the Columbia, the Paramount, the Grand, the Majestic, the Bijou."[11] Even Amana residents escaped the colonies' confines to see D. W. Griffith's *Birth of a Nation* when it played in Marengo.

Legitimating such new behaviors—driving automobiles, going to movies and roadside dance halls, bobbing one's hair or smoking cigarettes (which were illegal in Iowa until 1921)—were new cultural values and norms. Indulgence itself was no longer a sin but a sign of independence. As the immortal Iowan Muriel Hanford, better known as "the Peacock Girl," said, "You can't beat fun!"[12] Buying on credit was no longer a sign of shaky character but showed a modern outlook. Following that, allowing one's (middle-class) wife to work was tolerable if it promoted more purchases of refrigerators and washing machines.[13] One did one's best to live in style today, even if that meant not saving quite so much for tomorrow. Such was the case in Muncie, Indiana, Robert and Helen Lynd's "Middletown."[14] And such was the case in the Iowa county seat of Marengo.

MARENGO

A good point from which to trace the new consumerism as it affected this county seat is the year 1860, when the railroad finally connected little Marengo to Iowa City, to Chicago, to the nation. To some extent the railroad brought both life and death to the town, allowing Marengo products to be transported out, channeling a wide variety of goods into the community, and providing escape to large cities for those bored or frustrated with country life. Amana life had compared well with life on the outside when consumer goods were scarce everywhere and the security Amana residents enjoyed was hard to find elsewhere. It compared less well, however, as social life on the outside became more organized and as fancy eastern goods were shipped into Marengo stores. The change in goods and services available to Iowa County residents at Marengo is well summed up in an account published in an 1881 history of Iowa County:

The first store in Marengo was kept by William Downard in 1847. It was two blocks west of the square in a log building which served at once for a store and dwelling. The most of the traffic was with the Indians and those who were looking up claims. . . . All his goods could have been hauled in a one-horse wagon and were valued at about $300. What a change 33 years has wrought! Then a few articles hung on pegs driven into the logs and a few groceries and plugs of tobacco, now large store rooms filled with stocks of merchandise valued at from $10,000 to $60,000 surround the public square. There are now four large general stores, three dry goods stores, three hardware stores, and a great variety of other interests.[15]

By 1881 the board of trade was organized and the business directory listed "twelve grocery stores, eight saloons, four drug stores, four restaurants, eight firms of lawyers, six doctors, nine general stores, six shoe stores, and a complete list of other business firms." Few copies of early Marengo newspapers are still in existence, but a sampling of advertisements from 1866—the first year available—1903, and 1924 indicates the changing goods and services available.

The Marengo Progressive Republican of 3 February 1866 included advertisements for a range of services, among them those of a milliner—"Her work is always promptly done. . . . Ladies from the neighboring towns and the country are invited to give her a call"—two wagon makers—"Plows mended and sharpened, horse shoeing and all the best kinds of blacksmithing"—and finally one gentleman "who suffered for years from Nervous Disability, Premature Decay, and all the effects of youthful indiscretion," who for "the sake of suffering humanity" and a few dollars would tell of his cures. The general store was proud to note its eastern connections—"dry-goods carefully selected from the best eastern houses of New York, Boston, and Philadelphia"—and range of goods, including:

Flannels, Cloth, Muslin, Calicos, Alpacas, Mousselin, . . . Men's and Boys' Boots and shoes, fine and coarse. Undershirts and Drawers, Linen and Paper collars . . . Buck and Kid Gloves . . . Woolen and Cotton Hose. . . . Also, an extensive stock of Choice Groceries, Coffee, Tea and Sugar, Loaf, Crushed, Fair and Brown. Tobacco, Soap, Candles, . . . Starch, Sinnamon [sic], Cloves, Pepper, Nutmeg, Allspice, . . . Rope, Yarn and Twine. Wooden Ware. Tubs, Buckets, Pails, Washboards, and bowls. . . . We have adopted the cash system: and principle, of quick sales and small profits and will sell lower than any clothing dry goods and grocery establishment in the West.

By 1903, however, considerable specialization and extension had occurred in the consumer economy, so that the clothing, dry goods, and grocery establishment gave way to more specialized businesses. The gentleman who suffered from nervous disability yielded to an M.D., albeit one still offering relief from neuralgia and impotence; the muslins and calicos were pushed aside for silk and velour coats:

Women's Coats and Jackets. Smart Effects, Latest Style . . . The Long Silk Coat, The Velour Coat, The Novelty Jacket . . . Some Fur Specials . . . Sable, Fox, Mink, Martin, Opossum, Nutria, Beaver, Electric Seal, Black Bear . . . Henry Gode Big Corner Store. Phone 77.

Yet even more dramatic changes were to come, for by 1924 both the movies and the automobile had come to Marengo. In the last week of January that year the Strand movie theater was showing a new film every two nights, including Jackie Coogan in *Oliver Twist* and Dorothy Gish in *Fury*. Automobile ownership was now possible for many young men in the county. In 1924 a fancy new Studebaker sedan was priced at $1,495 ("Quality cars . . . built to endure—to give lasting satisfaction"), but a new Ford was by comparison a "striking value—at $295."

AMANA REACTION

The Amana trustees were not blind to these changes or to the attraction new consumer goods held for the Amana members. As early as the 1880s the trustees began their criticism of such worldly goods and individualism, as is reflected in the following list of items and practices banned by the trustees and the dates on which they were first mentioned:

Greeting cards	March, 1883
Outside newspapers	March, 1883
Birthday celebrations	April, 1889
Music in church	August, 1889
Wedding celebrations	July, 1891
Christmas celebrations	December, 1893

Card playing	January, 1894
Noisy celebrations on	
New Year's and the Fourth of July	January, 1894
Tricycles	August, 1894
Expensive baby carriages	August, 1894
New clothing fashions	November, 1894
Bicycles	July, 1896
Drinking parties	November, 1897
Wear hair down, not in cap	July, 1898
Open vests	December, 1899 [16]

Such inroads only increased, however, and the last generation to grow up under the old system can remember the forbidden delights of the two pre-Change decades. Lucky colonists arranged trips to Marengo, even luckier ones managed longer stays with relatives living on the outside. At South Amana one woman said:

Oh yes, going to Marengo for an ice cream was a big treat. But once Mother went to Marengo and had *both* an ice cream *and* went to a movie—Booth Tarkington. She had such a good time, but she was so afraid someone would find out.

Another woman confirmed the excitement of "going to town"—not just for colonists but for neighboring farmers as well:

Every so often we would go for an outing to Marengo, five miles away. That took a long time by horse and buggy. We would go look in shops, maybe get an ice cream cone. Then every summer I would spend a week with relatives who had a farm. I loved that. They had little girls my age, and like farmers all over they would go down to town on Saturday nights and we might get an ice cream cone. They didn't sell ice cream like that in Amana when I was little, only later.

Yet you hardly had to journey away from the Amanas for a taste of the outside: Sears and Roebuck would bring it to you. Said one man who later would be much involved in the change that made such goods both legal and achievable:

With the Sears and Roebuck catalogs coming in, the children would sit down and pick out what they wanted for Christmas. And if you had no money there was no way you could get it for them. So you had to think of a way to get some money. Those who were very good with woodworking could make up an extra piece of furniture. Those of us who had children saw them leafing through the catalogs and picking out what they wanted for Christmas. I too had to think of a way to get it for them. We had a garden, as did everyone, so I sold some produce, and we also had pear trees, and so I canned and sold the pears.

Young girls in particular rebelled against the staid Amana garb, preferring bright colors to the somber blacks and grays, and hoped that in their "nice" dresses they would look as attractive and as modern as the outside girls. Such efforts were seldom appreciated by their elders, but then, who cared?

By the time I was a teenager I had a lot of nice dresses, though many were hand-me-downs. We wore the Amana costume for church only. And then one day I bobbed my hair. I wasn't the first. Henrietta and my other friends had all bobbed their hair. They all told me not to, because they all liked my beautiful long, thick hair, but one evening I left for Marengo with my friends saying I would get it cut, and I came home with it cut. And I told them, "Henrietta had her hair cut." And they said, "But Henrietta doesn't have such beautiful hair."

Yet the young were not the only ones to suffer temptations: for the adults they simply came in bigger packages. The largest and the most destructive of communal life was the automobile. Barbara Yambura provides a delightful description of the fascination the arrival of an automobile occasioned in her account of Amana life, *A Change and a Parting*:

Henry and I were already far ahead of the others as we ran down the hill. This was a brand new, shiny black Ford, similar to Dr. Breck's but a later model. The canvas top was neatly folded back and the machine looked as though it had just been dusted and polished.

"Will you take us for a ride?" I wanted to know.

"Sure," said Uncle John, "But only in the country. We can't go near the village because the elders might have something to say." . . .

That was the beginning of many rides we had with Uncle John. For the rest of the season he kept the car hidden out along the country roads. Finally, he decided that everyone knew he had it so he brought it in to the barns, the inference being that the head of the farms needed a car.[17]

The farm managers, along with the doctors and trustees, were the first to justify their desire for cars, but soon everyone who could afford one had one. The money for such extravagances came in most cases from small, secret nest eggs that had been

Table 2: Population Data for the Amana
Society 1855–1934, Five-Year Periods

Period	Total Population	Percentage Change	Births	Deaths	Net Migration
1855	74		7	0	0
1856–60	572	+670	31	19	+486
1861–65	1,240	+117	83	85	+670
1866–70	1,466	+18	110	93	+209
1871–75	1,598	+9	137	137	+132
1876–80	1,721	+8	118	126	+131
1881–85	1,732	+0.6	99	128	−40
1886–90	1,688	−2.5	103	130	—
1891–95	1,717	+1.7	124	146	—
1896–1900	1,766	+2.9	178	127	−2
1901–5	1,770	+0.2	185	137	−44
1906–10	1,655	−6.5	143	142	−116
1911–15	1,568	−5.2	109	137	−59
1916–20	1,440	−8.2	120	121	−127
1921–25	1,385	−3.8	104	103	−26
1926–30	1,378	−0.5	109	105	−11
1931–35	1,458	+5.5	79	103	−100

Source: Andelson, "Communalism and Change," p. 449.

built up for just such forbidden pleasures. Photographs from this
period convey a restlessness, especially on the part of the young.
The adolescent girls in their fanciful dresses are set off by more
than years from grandmothers still true to the old Amana garb.
The amusements are simple: girls dress up as boys, down to the
cigar, or mimic lovers behind the washhouse. The real excitement, however, is clearly the visit from outside relatives: eight
men pose proudly in and around a magnificent Franklin Pierce
Arrow.

Indeed, it was the automobile that made tourist visits to the
Amanas a daily experience. Tourists would drive slowly through

the villages, perhaps stopping to have their pictures taken with some Inspirationists before having lunch at the hotel. Village stores offered special goods to be purchased by tourists only. In addition, with people who had left the community coming back to visit their relatives, those who stayed got firsthand word on chances and conditions in the world beyond.

These visiting relatives formed only part of a larger group of emigrants. Although the population fluctuated somewhat throughout the later half of the nineteenth century and the early twentieth century, births usually compensated for both deaths and emigrations in the long run. Starting in 1905, however, a steady and inexorable loss of population resulted from the increased emigrations and the associated decline in the birthrate, since many of those leaving were of childbearing age (table 2). Again, the trustees turned to the platform provided by the *Inspirations-Historie* to condemn these deviants:

At this time a number of families as well as some young adult individuals left the community. Also the Family F—— of Homestead, who managed the hotel, which was profitable and useful, emigrated to the outside world. With most of them the chief reason was love of vanity and worldliness and lack of grounding in true faith and obedience, and with others, the great falsehood and infidelity were at fault and they could not resist.

Nonetheless, young people continued to leave the community, though clearly not all for the same reason. Many left for what they sensed to be greater opportunities, some for education, some for religious considerations; some were drawn like Sister Carrie to the excitement of city lights. These individuals, crossing the boundary between pietist commune and the broader society, reflected at once the problems of the first and the promises of the second.

Some Who Left

CHAPTER 8

Curiously, my own family presents an excellent case study of the reasons young people left Amana and what awaited them in the outside world. Indeed, someone laying odds in the pre-Change years might have bet that the four Ehrmann girls would be among those leaving the Amanas. They had all grown up in West Amana, where the town of Marengo, seven miles distant, was almost as close as the central village of Amana six miles the other way. Their father, a cabinetmaker, occasionally filled special orders for neighboring farmers, who of course spoke English. They had relatives on the outside, including a photographer in Marengo and an uncle who drove a hearse in Chicago. All these family reasons counted, but the girls also found reasons of their own.

Selma, the oldest, was the first to go, at the age of twenty-two. Although an "ideal citizen" and an exceptionally hard worker, she felt opportunity lay elsewhere. Her first jobs were the typical ones a young Amana woman might find on the outside—working on a farm and in a hospital in Iowa City, doing housework in Des Moines: with her first check she bought a glamorous maroon plush coat. But she did not want to clean homes or hospitals. She wanted to make hats:

I was always good with my hands. I was in Cedar Rapids on my way to Chicago, but my friend said, "Oh, Selma, Chicago's no place for a girl like you. Chicago's a bad town." So I went to Milwaukee.

In Milwaukee I got off the train and there was a woman there from the Traveler's Aid, and she spotted me right away and said she was going to take care of me. I wanted to go to the YWCA, but no, she told me to go with her and she took me to a house where, actually, there were a lot of prostitutes. She said, "Now I know you're not that type of girl, but you stay here until I check out your background." The next day another woman came back and said, "This is no place for you," and she got me a room in a girls' home.

Then I got a job in a wholesale millinery place in Milwaukee. I stayed for a while, but I still wanted to go to Chicago. So I went to Chicago, and Frieda came up later. But then we went to Detroit. I had a hard time finding work. . . . So I decided to go back to Chicago.

I worked for a while at Marshall Field's in the workshop, but then I got laid off. . . . Then one of the girls knew of a woman with a hat shop who needed a girl. She hired me. The pay wasn't much, but gosh, you didn't need much then. So I worked for her, though after a while her mother and sister convinced her to go back to California, so she left me the shop. There wasn't much there, but that's how I got my first hat shop. . . .

So I had my shop and I made custom hats.

Frieda, the next oldest, was the next to leave, also in her early twenties. She, like Selma, had spent several years cooking and scrubbing in the communal kitchens and looked to the greater opportunities beyond:

It was in 1923 that I left Amana. Why did I leave? I don't know. You get some crazy ideas in your head. I wanted to see the world.

I went to Des Moines and worked for a family where Selma was already doing housework. I took care of the children. I've always enjoyed that. Then I worked for another family, then a hospital.

Then after two or three years we left for Detroit. I went to beauty school there because I had always enjoyed fooling around with hair—you certainly couldn't do that in Amana. Then I started working for the shop. Mrs. Ford was one of my clients. When she died the papers said she was the richest woman in the United States, and I told all my friends I had done the hair of the richest woman.

I liked Detroit. It was a big city, but you could walk down the street, meet two or three people you knew on the way. . . .

I left Amana because I could see no future for me there. I was in Detroit when I heard of the Change, and I was glad. They certainly did well to change.

Then my mother jumped out of line, leaving ahead of her older sister Rose. Her leaving was particularly traumatic, because she was only sixteen at the time:

I suspected even before leaving school in Amana that I wouldn't like kitchen work. I hated it from the first day. They sat me down to peeling potatoes, cleaning knives and forks, preparing vegetables. Oh, how I hated it. I couldn't see myself doing that all my life—it wasn't anywhere near as much fun as learning. Slowly the idea grew on me that I could make it on the outside.

So one afternoon I left. Lucille helped me walk to the train station with my baggage. I had put an advertisement in the Des Moines papers for someone who wanted a schoolgirl to clean, and sure enough someone responded to it, sight unseen. I think I had more nerve than sense.

I went to work for this lady, then another. Then I went to the YWCA and asked if they could help me find another situation. They called back in a few days with Mabel's name.

She took an interest in me and my plans. I worked for her while I went through high school. Then I went to the telephone company. Soon I became dissatisfied there too. One of the girls working there had been to college. She told me, "You can do it."

Go to college she eventually did, working her way through and becoming a campus leader. Local newspapers would occasionally do a feature story, with one describing her as follows:

Miss Ehrmann's ancestry goes back to the hills of Germany near the province of Alsace. Her dark hair, dark complexion and sparkling eyes are suggestive of southern Europeans, but her clear, strong voice is distinctly Teutonic. She has no trace of dialect in her English, and despite her fast ties to the old world, she maintains that she is a true American. Her freedom-loving, independent qualities prove that she is right.

The story of the former young girl "garbed in the demurest of plain gingham dresses," a girl who then spoke only German but who now led the Cornell College debate team, was good copy for the newspapers and served to reinforce significant American myths. Here was support for the image of a great melting pot deriving its distinctive character from the ingredients of all nations, but showing the superiority of the "American way of life" over all others. This "freedom-loving" young woman who cherishes the old ways but chooses the new, this popular collegian formerly locked in a "backward" religion, before whom all doors now stand open, served to shore up the myth of the American dream.[1] Such themes as these would be sounded again as the community itself faced the choice between the old and new.

With three of the sisters gone, the last also left, along with her husband Carl, motivated this time by a curious admixture of religion and dental problems:

ROSE: It was because of Christian Science. We didn't have that in Amana. You see, Mother was very, very ill in 1918. The doctors had given up hope. Uncle Charley said to us, "I don't know what to say."

But then later he said he'd heard of Christian Science, and he thought it might be worth a try. So Frieda had a friend in Homestead, who got in touch with a practitioner in Iowa City. And you know, after the first treatment Mother could eat again. She lived to 1947—and this was in 1918. After that she never took any more medicine. It just made her sick. The more pills and medicine she took the sicker she got.

Then we got married in 1921. In 1927 my teeth were so bad—they had messed them up in Amana—that I had to get them fixed in Des Moines. Lissette and Mrs. Poff would come down to visit and they drove me back.

CARL: Mrs. Poff used to kid me always, saying, "Charley, when are you going to leave and come up to Des Moines?" This time I said, "If Rose leaves with you Sunday, I'm coming up Monday."

That night I had a terrible night. I tossed and turned. I asked, "Am I going to leave or am I going to stay?" The next morning I got up and told my mother I was going to Des Moines. She said, "You're crazy."

I took the train from South Amana to Des Moines. This was when Mrs. Poff was trying to buy a car. So I get to her house, she was out with a salesman buying the Dodge, so I sat down. When she came back riding in her new car she looked out and said, "My God, there's Charley sitting on the step!"

So Mrs. Poff said to me, "Charley, what are you going to do now?" and I said, "Well, I guess I'll try to get a job. Do you know of anything?" She thought maybe her contractor, the man who had done some work for her, might have a job, and he did. He said, "You can start Monday." I said, "That's a little too soon." But I went home to Amana, got my things together, took care of the house, and left. That was a very hard decision, but sometimes you've just got to make a radical decision.

Unlike these four and the many others who, when they left the

Amanas, left for good, some, like the following man, tried their luck on the outside but then returned to the villages:

I left when I was sixteen. The elders decided I should work as a clerk in the general store here, but I didn't want to do it. I said I was going to leave, and they said, you won't get a job, no one will hire you. But my father and grandmother talked it over and decided I could go, as long as my grandmother was in good health and didn't need me. We had relatives down in Kansas City, so I went down there and moved in with them.

I worked first in one factory, then I worked in a candy factory, but the smell! I couldn't stand it, it gets to your stomach. I worked there for only three days, then went to a job where I had to work nine hours a day, plus three evenings a week. On top of that it took me one and a half hours to get to work, so you can see I didn't have much time for sleep or for anything else. So I quit that job. That evening as I was going home I saw some boys my age running around. Turned out they were Western Union messenger boys. So I went into the office, they asked me some questions, and then sent me over to the other office to get fitted for a uniform.

After that my family decided they wanted me closer to home, so I started working on a farm nearby. Then my grandmother was ailing, so in 1920 I came home.

In all these accounts we see the importance of the family mediating the pull of community on the individual, providing a countervailing allegiance and a source of support. The family also could be an obstacle to a person's forsaking the community: the four sisters all expressed sorrow at leaving their family, but leave they did. In this last case the family first legitimated the young man's trying his luck on the outside, but then called him back into the communal fold.

Despite increasing liberalization, there was still shame attached to the returnee who wanted to be accepted back into the group:

In order to be accepted into the community, I had to get up in front of the church on Sunday afternoon, turn, and face the congregation. Believe me, *everyone* was in church that Sunday. Everyone. I had to say that I had been wrong to leave, and ask to be admitted back into the community. There was really no question that I would be accepted, but still, I was nervous. My knees were shaking.

By way of comparison, it is interesting to note that among the Hutterites certain families are known as "weak" families: it is their sons and daughters who can be expected to leave the communities. As in Amana, among the Hutterites some young people leave for wider opportunities, some for greater excitement, some because of disputes with the Hutterite authorities. Every effort is made to encourage the apostate to return to the fold, and those living on the outside are still allowed to visit relatives within the Hutterite settlements.

The treatment appears to be far different among the Amish. While the Amish differ among themselves in strictness, many "shun" those attached to alternate beliefs and practices. Many communities excommunicate members who sin too deeply or refuse to repent. Some shunned members, however, may be readmitted if they kneel and beg forgiveness of their group and the presiding bishop. Thus, while the dominant pattern among Hutterites on this question of group boundaries is not far different from that practiced in Amana in the 1910s and 1920s, the Amish continue to maintain far stricter segregation between themselves and the world.[2]

In Amana, while some risked the failures, others dreamed but dared not risk. One woman who stayed to make her life in Amana surprised even her good friend when she spoke of her earlier indecision:

I did toy with the idea of leaving once. My very best friend ran away when she was only fourteen, to work on a farm. She and I and another girl had been very close. I was tempted to leave then, but I didn't. I was too timid.

The majority decided Amana was their home and stayed. Devotion to family and church figured in many a decision, as in the case of one man who is now an elder:

I had never any doubt nor question about staying in Amana. I am a firm believer in the Amana church. I have a daughter living in Illinois. Every time my wife and I go to visit they drive us around to show us the nice houses and my daughter says she wants us to move there and live close to them. But I would never leave Amana.

And another man in Middle Amana:

I never thought of leaving. For me the Amana church has always been the truest, the most real.

Yet even most of those who remained came to open their minds to the outside. In time they transformed their lives by dismantling their communal structure to follow modern society's directives and to seek out its benefits.

The Orchestration of Change

CHAPTER 9

NOT far east of Amana, at West Branch, lies the birthplace of Herbert Hoover. In the spring of 1932 Hoover was campaigning for a second term as president, and few doubted that central to the election would be his apparent failure to end the Depression. While in Washington the president and his aides sat desperately trying to work out an economic solution to the nation's troubles, back home in Iowa Amana colonists were also debating their economic future.

It was clear to many colonists that a crisis point had been reached and that a choice, however painful, would have to be made. Indeed, some residents recall discussing reorganization as early as 1915, but the idea was given up because no solution appeared to problems revolving around proper care of the elderly, who had spent their lives contributing to the old system and would have difficulty adapting to any new regime. Thus the idea of change was not new when, in 1931, it became obvious from the financial side alone that the community would have to face the hard facts. Still holding it back after all these years, however, was an injunction of Christian Metz: "As truly as I live, says the Lord, it is at no time my will to dissolve the ties of the community . . . or to suffer its dissolution, either through artful devices, skill, and diplomacy or through cunning and power of men." Despite the decline in spiritual and communal fervor, some of the older members still took Metz's admonition to heart and opposed any move that would threaten Amana's communal structure and heritage. Thus something that had begun as a strategy to deal with external conditions and changes had over time become legitimated as an integral part of the religious myth.

However, it was increasingly obvious to most of the leaders, as to the members, that change was needed. The first actual step was taken in March 1931 when the board of trustees moved to appoint a committee of four to explain to each village the problems faced by the community as a whole. Each village was to elect members to what became known as the "Committee of Forty-seven." In addition, at this time a letter was sent to each community member asking for responses to the following questions:

1. Is it, in your opinion, possible to go back to the old lifestyle of denial wholly and completely, as it is prescribed, and are you and your family willing to tread this path without reservation?

2. Is it, in your opinion, possible that by reorganization (which is described as fully as can be at this time in the accompanying letter), the building-up of our community can be effected according to Article V of our present Constitution, and are you and your family willing to present your plans and views before the Committee and then to assist in carrying out the plan approved by the Trustees and the majority of our brothers and sisters?

Of the 917 letters mailed out, 900 were returned. All the villages except Middle Amana voted overwhelmingly for a change.[1] The breakdown by village was as follows, with villages on the railroad, and thus most exposed to the "outside," voting most strongly for a change.

Amana	93%
Middle Amana	24.5
High Amana	52
West Amana	92
South Amana	96
Homestead	96
East Amana	66

Of the total responses, 74 percent were for a reorganization.[2]

Following this vote, the Committee of Forty-seven took it upon itself to explore possibilities and develop plans that would be both feasible and acceptable to the community. The problems they faced were considerable. As one present-day elder recalls them:

First of all you had to be absolutely fair, develop plans which would be fair to all. Then you had to decide who would live where. Some were living in nice sandstone houses, some in wooden houses. Those in wooden houses could have bid for the sandstone, but there was not one case of their doing so. Living in the houses for so long as we did, the houses were viewed as the "Noes'" house or the "Geigers'." We had the question of which of the shops would be abandoned or phased out. We did this as painlessly as possible. We told people that in two weeks we would turn the key. They were told to look around to find a job, or we would offer to find one for them.

Then the senior citizen group would be penniless. So the way it was done—they would redeem some of the shares and live on the proceeds of redemption. The commonplace then was $50, the preferred stock $65. And it was the Depression so $65 would go quite far.

What would happen to the elderly still troubled many members of the community, for among the benefits of the old system was the care and security it gave the aged: there was now much concern whether these people who had spent their lives contributing to the old system would be adequately rewarded by the new.

As discussion continued, it soon became apparent that forty-seven was an unwieldy number for such a task, so a smaller "Committee of Twenty-three" was selected from its ranks, then later from that another "Committee of Ten" to outline the proposed reorganization plan. Meetings of the larger two committees were held through the rest of 1931 to work out the details and legalities of the plan. On 2 January 1932 the plan was adopted by the Committee of Forty-seven with a vote of thirty-nine for, six opposed.[3]

The plan was then presented to the community at large, and, despite numerous fears and the remaining ties to the past, 90 percent of Amana members voted for the Change. As one who cast her vote remembers, "There was no choice. There was no going back."

In the final plan, two distinct societies were established: the

Amana Church Society, with responsibility for the religious, benevolent, and charitable activities of the community, and the Amana Society, which became a stock company organized for profit. A board of directors was to be named by a representative committee and voted on by the stockholders. There were to be three types of stock: class A, class B, and preferred. Each member of the Society received one share of class A stock and additional shares based on years spent working for the community. This stock carried voting rights. Each member also received a number of prior distributive shares of capital stock that provided a noncumulative dividend each year. Class B stock was to be issued only on a vote of the stockholders, while preferred stock could be issued by the board of directors without such a vote. Neither stock, in contrast to class A stock, carried voting privileges. Awarding shares for years spent working for the community meant the elderly would be well provided for. Members could also sell some of their stock to buy their houses. As for the other branch of the reorganized society, the Amana Church Society, the community's old board of trustees became its first governing board. The Church Society controls church and school buildings as well as cemeteries, where class A stockholders have the right to free burial.[4]

The solution arrived at was not unlike that reached fifty years earlier in New York State when Oneida made its historic transition from commune to corporation. The causes leading up to communal demise in that case had been somewhat different, reflecting Oneida's different social structure and composition. John Humphrey Noyes, Oneida's charismatic leader, had helped undermine his own theology by deemphasizing the transcendent or spiritual aspects and seizing upon the new field of social studies as an area for community inquiry. Second, and perhaps not unrelated to this deemphasis of the sacred, was the challenge mounted to Noyes's right to pick the "first husbands" who would initiate the young girls into the Oneida form of group marriage. Out of this controversy a serious schism developed that, combined with pressure against group marriage from the outside, critically undermined the basis for communal living.[5] In the plans that went into effect 1 January 1880, shares were dis-

tributed to members on the basis of original financial contribution and years of service. Members could, as in Amana, then opt
to work for the corporation at a very low initial pay that, as in
Amana, was soon increased. It was only considerably later, in
1905, that the community, under the leadership of J. Pierre-
pont Noyes, started producing the now-famous line of Oneida
silverware.[6]

The process of economic transformation in Amana needed a
"midwife" from the outside: one Arthur Barlow, former examiner
for the Minnesota State Banking Department, was named by the
colonies as their business manager. Barlow took charge of the
community's economic situation from 1932 to 1944 and was also
involved in 1950–52 when the Amana Society charter had to be
renewed.[7]

Barlow has written of his role in this process, and particularly
striking is his perception of the financial irrationalities of the old
system.[8] The community leaders, for example, at first resisted
Barlow's suggestion that a public accountant be hired—they
were suspicious, perhaps, of inviting in still another outsider. In
addition, in trying to assess the community's liabilities Barlow
found that no central accounting existed; he had to discover in
what bank in what town each separate village maintained its records. Further, when Barlow took charge there were fifty-nine
separate businesses in the Amanas: he moved quickly to close
several of the harness shops and watchmakers, the soap works,
shoemaker shops, and basket shops, which had not been economically viable. He also had trouble convincing the individual
businessmen to adopt a modern accounting system of sales and
cash on hand.

It was decided that everyone would start out earning only ten
cents an hour, since capital was sorely lacking, but that credit
would be extended. It was hoped (as did come to pass) that this
salary would soon be increased. There was some ill feeling among
the more highly trained members that their services, so well paid
on the outside, would not be similarly rewarded by the colonies.
But they agreed to give the new plan a try.

With this reorganization social change finally came to the
Amanas. Their isolation—physical, economic, and cultural—

slowly chipped away for decades past, was all but gone. How did the people themselves experience this radical change from religious commune to capitalist enterprise? One elderly woman remembers what it was like to wake up that first morning after the Change:

The Change went into effect overnight, from a Saturday night to a Sunday. When you woke up that Sunday morning, you just felt you had seen the passing of an era.

I think we were scared. You see, everything had always been taken care of. For the elderly especially you never had to worry where your next meal was coming from, if you'd have enough money, or who would take care of you, someone would be assigned. Yes, there were a lot of benefits, but if you ask around, they wouldn't want to go back to the old way. I wouldn't.

After the Change I was assigned to work in a cooperative garden. We raised a lot of onions for sale on the outside, tried some other things. The first couple of years weren't too good. We started off being paid 10¢ an hour, which wasn't much, but then you didn't need much.

Another man, then in his twenties, faced this Great Change with his energies and ambitions afire:

Personally, I was so eager to get going I set right to work at the bakery. We were working to establish contacts with the outside world, which were now more necessary than ever.

The story of one particular Amana resident demonstrates the enthusiasm and energy with which many Amana people welcomed the challenge of going it alone. George Foerstner, a young man who had already made something of a name for himself as a salesman, got the idea that the local farmers needed some type of beer cooler. With his friend Otto Zuber, Foerstner built such a beverage cooler, and the product soon had remarkable success, despite Foerstner's limited education, youth (age twenty-four), and small capital.[9] That was the start of Amana Refrigeration, Incorporated, which now markets Amana refrigerators, freezers, and microwave ovens the world over.

The Interpretation of Change

I F there ever was a period when harsh reality gave the lie to the American dream, the Depression surely was such a time. A people's hopes of prosperity and progress, legitimated and encouraged by their cultural myths, were confronted by the stock market collapse, mortgage foreclosures, and massive unemployment. In this period of national crisis, the national myths would be sorely tested. But they would not be rejected outright.

Even before the crash and the Depression's onset, industrialization and urbanization had already created an America far different from the one celebrated in its myths. Although in 1890 the frontier was officially declared closed, the myth of the frontiersman has endured. By 1920 America was predominantly an urban nation. Still the myth of the agrarian ideal, a Jeffersonian vision of a nation of yeoman farmers, continued to provide many with an image of what they were or should be: self-sufficient, morally upright, and independent. Indeed, given such contradictions between myth and political reality, it has appeared to some scholars that the further America moved from the images contained in its myths, the more firmly it held to them. Richard Hofstadter, for example, believes that:

The more commercial this society became the more reason it found to cling in its imagination to the noncommercial agrarian values. The more farming as a self-sufficient way of life was abandoned for farming as a business, the more merit men found in what was being left behind. And the more rapidly the farmers' sons moved into the towns, the more nostalgic the whole culture became about its rural past.[1]

While some people clung to these myths through hardship, others perceived the disjuncture between the inspiration provided by myth and the hard facts of economic survival. Thus, according to Henry Nash Smith:

Given a break in the upward curve of economic progress for the Western farmer, the myth would become a mockery, offering no consolation and serving only to intensify the sense of outrage on the part of men and women who discovered that labor in the fields did not bring the cheerful comfort promised them by so many prophets of the future of the West.[2]

But the shattering of old promises did not stop the prophets of popular culture from making new ones. While serious literature such as Steinbeck's *Grapes of Wrath* and *Of Mice and Men* dealt with the suffering and disillusionment, popular culture—magazines, movies, the many "success books"—promised not just that good times were around the corner but also quite literally that money was waiting on the street. The media in the 1930s thus strove to shore up the myths that legitimated the political and economic structure. Newspapers, books, and magazines gave personal advice, created fictional examples of successful individuals in advertisements and short stories, and presented real-life examples whenever possible.[3] As part of this search for testimonials, one of the items that came to newspaper editors as historical fact, but was transformed by them into cultural myth, was the organizational change then occurring in the Amana Colonies.

Newspapers across the nation carried news of Amana's Great Change. Indeed, the transformation from communal sect to capitalist corporation right in the depths of the Depression struck many chords. But the notes sounded were not always true to the actual events. Often they were closer to happenings outside the community's borders. From the collected newspaper articles two major themes emerge: one political, one cultural. Curiously, the religious significance of the event was hardly considered. Let us listen once again to word of the Change, this time as it was heard and given cultural meaning by the larger society.

COMMUNISM'S BEST CHANCE

In 1932, with the big news of Depression economics, the presidential campaign of Hoover versus Roosevelt, and the Lindbergh kidnapping still in the headlines, it may seem strange that readers could work up much enthusiasm over the fate of this small sect. Indeed, Amana rarely, at least outside Iowa, stole the front page from these other items. Yet it was considered newsworthy, largely as a negative example. In these Depression days many were turning to communism as the economic solution. Some were arguing that the Depression signaled capitalism's demise and that the nation had best turn to Russia for new inspiration.[4]

It was, in fact, precisely because communism was proving attractive to many that its rejection was so important to others. Amana served their purpose well, for—as the reporters argued— if communism had failed these simple, God-fearing Iowa farmers, then it would fail everyone everywhere. That was clearly the message in headlines such as:

> COMMUNIST COLONY GOES CAPITALIST
> US's Oldest Experiment of This Nature
> Decides Plan Is a Failure
> (*Rochester Times-Union,*
> Rochester, New York, 25 April 1932)

> "PERFECT" COMMUNIST COLONY DROPS
> DOCTRINES FOR CAPITALISTIC PLAN
> (*Pasadena Post,* 17 January 1933)

> NATION'S ONLY COMMUNIST UTOPIA
> TURNS CAPITALISTIC AND PROSPERS
> Roused by Slump, Amana Society
> Becomes a Rich Industrial Hive
> (*Philadelphia Record,* 18 June 1933)[5]

The message that communism—and indeed all social welfare policies—was doomed to fail was often pointed directly toward Washington. This was especially true in articles appearing several years after the Change, hence also several years after the 1932 election of Franklin Delano Roosevelt. Conservative midwestern newspapers such as the *Chicago Journal of Commerce* would repeatedly dredge up the Amana story and what they saw as its object lesson, a lesson intended for Roosevelt himself, for his "meddlesome" wife Eleanor, and for the eastern brain trusters such as Rexford Tugwell who were proposing what to these midwestern journalists appeared as a socialist solution: un-American, irreligious, and bad for business. From the *Chicago Journal of Commerce*, 21 September 1934:

A DIFFERENT NEW DEAL

The Communist Amana Communities Switch to Individualism and Corporate Structure; Recovery in Progress

While Washington brain trusters are struggling with problems involved in our national New Deal and national recovery program, out here among the fertile fields of Iowa an equally zealous group is involved in a similar problem, but the reverse of our national one. Here one of the oldest and most successful communistic communities in the world is undergoing a transition from communism to individualism. Nationally the least we can say is that the tendency is in the opposite direction. . . .

The new management is optimistic. They believe they see the way clear to better times. . . . They take a keen interest in the national trends toward socialism or communism, but they think that in the Amanas they have reached the best combination of capitalism, communism and individualism. They point out that Henry Ford's idea of factory and farm combination is no different from the system they are following and that the national government's experiments are not the same. . . .

Perhaps our governmental leaders could do worse than to study some of the results obtained in this "New Deal" of a one-time truly communistic society.

From the *Moline Daily Dispatch*, an editorial dated 23 December 1936, after summarizing the historic change, made the following comment on its significance:

Of course, [the colonists] did not know then about Professor Tugwell, and we wonder if Tugwell knew about them. Was he so bound up with study and eulogy of the Godless communism of Russia that he overlooked a communism that had been in operation in his own country for seventy-five years on a religious basis?

We suspect that these Amana people could have enlightened Professor Tugwell and Mrs. Roosevelt greatly concerning "subsistence homesteads" and "communal farms" and "communal industries," and perhaps incidentally might have saved the taxpayers large sums of money.

The editorial went on to list what it saw as the differences between this "God-fearing brand of communism and that of the Russian stripe:"

It was simply and successfully communistic for many years, but not along the Russian pattern. Instead of undertaking to destroy God, the Amana people made religion the foundation of their community life. . . .

The Society differed from the Russian pattern also in that there was no dictatorship to thunder down at the populace. There was no "liquidation" of the farmers who had previously prospered. There was no censorship of the reading matter that circulated within the territory. There was no army of spies. . . .

Conditions were ideal for an experiment with the system of communism and its "production for use," and these thrifty and religious people carried it on for seventy-five years.

Then they took a practical view of the thing and decided that the capitalistic system under which profits were paid according to the stock held and wages paid according to the work done was the system under which they best could pursue their business of farming and milling.

"They took a practical view of the thing." Two hundred and twenty years of history as a dissenting sect, a communal enclave—a history filled with intriguing twists and unsuspected outcomes—is thus transmogrified to fit the ideological demands of the political moment. As is so often true of myth, such articles suggested there was never any real alternative to the social structure American society developed or to the values it espoused: witness the failure of this one small attempt at a different solution.

But had communalism truly failed the Amana people? In 1932 were they that much worse off than their neighboring Iowa farmers? Indeed, when we look outside the community borders the case is by no means as clear as the newspapers would have it. Compared with other midwestern farmers in that Depression year, the erstwhile communards do not come off badly.

In the summer of 1932, while the new Amana corporation was providing jobs for all residents who asked, farmers in western Iowa were dumping their milk cans onto the highways to protest the pitifully low prices paid them for the milk. Violence in places such as Sioux City was so great that the National Guard was called out to quell the farmers' rebellion. Elsewhere in Iowa and the neighboring states of Kansas, Nebraska, and the Dakotas, mortgage foreclosures were so common that farmers finally banded together to block farm sales. They bought farmland and machinery for ridiculously low sums, which went to the bank, then returned the farm to its owners. The Farm Holiday Association was active in organizing such protests and in taking the farmers' case directly to Washington in search of relief.[6]

In Amana, by contrast, all had the right to their homes, once communal property and now theirs mortgage-free. They had jobs, albeit at minimal pay; they had their shares in the new corporation; and they had, less concretely but still significantly, the support of their neighbors, who knew they were still all in it together. The Amana people had been wise enough not to discard their solidarity completely. Instead of opting for a "pure" form of capitalism, as many newspapers incorrectly interpreted their changeover plans, they chose a structure that would allow centralized control over Amana land and much of the economy but that also granted independence to those who wanted to find their work elsewhere and allowed all to choose their own consumption patterns and forms of sociability. Instead of becoming a typical middle American town, the Amanas became an atypical company town, with authority now vested not in the church's board of trustees, but in the corporation's board of trustees. Political reality was not, in brief, as neat as myth would make it.

THE MYTH OF THE GARDEN
VERSUS THE SELF-MADE MAN

The Amana story also struck a chord deeper than the political one, a chord that resonated with profound cultural longings. The Amana saga echoed a story many Americans had told about themselves since the nation's founding. Henry Nash Smith has referred to this story as the myth of the garden, a pastoral tale in which innocence and harmony are cherished yet ultimately are destroyed by forces impinging from the outside:

When the new economic and technological forces . . . had done their work, the garden was no longer a garden. But the image of an agricultural paradise in the West, embodying group memories of an earlier, a simpler, and it was believed, a happier state of society, long survived in American thought and politics.[7]

Several newspaper articles treated the old Amana as just such a garden, often expressing this in biblical phraseology. Barlow, the outside businessman hired to straighten out the Amana economy, was seen as a "new prophet." Beards magically appeared on the usually clean-shaven Amana men in references to "bearded elders," and communal members were seen as tempted, like the Israelites, by "gold and silver."

The colonists dressed, worshipped and reasoned alike, before the reorganization. Their standards of living were identical. Everything in the seven villages was owned and shared by all. No one possessed for himself a horse, cow, house, a garden spot, or even a dog.

For three quarters of a century residents of the Amanas used money only in business contacts with the outside world. They ate at a community table, received necessities of life from a community store, and abhorred the use of gold and silver.

Sociologists and economists cited the colonies as the world's most perfect example of Communistic success.—*Des Moines Register*, 2 August 1936

Idyllic as the picture seems, the myth of the unchanging garden was in conflict with another cherished national myth: the myth of opportunity and the self-made man. As Richard Hofstadter has pointed out, the same forces that created the agrarian ideal also unleashed "an entrepreneurial zeal probably without precedent in history, a rage for business, for profits, for opportunity, for advancement." He continues:

If the yeoman family was to maintain itself in the simple terms eulogized in the myth, it had to produce consistently a type of character that was satisfied with a traditional way of life. But the Yankee farmer, continually exposed to the cult of success that was everywhere around him, became inspired by a kind of personal dynamism which called upon the individual to surpass tradition. . . . Agrarian sentiment sanctified labor in the soil and the simple life, but the prevailing Calvinist atmosphere of rural life implied that virtue was rewarded, after all, with success and material goods.[8]

Thus in Amana, though the old communal structure had its claim upon the members, the greater force of this competing myth required a definition of human nature that would not be satisfied with stasis. It quickly fell to the young people to play the role of Eve and hunger after knowledge of the world and also after its goods:

It was a strange mingling of the old and the new that finally broke the Communistic system. Youths introduced to capitalism became restless when there was no jingle of money in their pockets after a week's work.—*Pasadena Post*, 17 January 1933

Undoubtedly the religious zeal in which the Amana community was founded supplied the motive power that kept it alive for so many years. That zeal is fading in the younger generation, and it is they who insisted on the quiet "revolution" which has now taken place.

Thus Amana, largest and richest of the surviving American experiments in communism, goes the way of Oneida, Harmony, Icaria, Zoar and Brook Farm, all conceived in a lofty idealism, and all wrecked on reefs of human frailty.—*Panama American*, 12 February 1933

"Modern women" were now to be found even within the colony's borders:

Young women of this strange colony, established seventy-five years ago, have already "gone modern" as regards bobbed hair and short skirts and there is a growing sentiment against the ban on electric lights, radios, games, music, and privately owned motor cars. . . .

One young woman said, "The old fogies threatened to expel us if we broke away from those hateful styles, but there were too many of us. Look around and you'll see that nearly all of the younger women wear short skirts and bobbed hair. We are free at last and we are going to stay free and be like other folks. They can't tell a younger woman that a woman's morality and Christianity depend on the way she wears her hair. We can go barelegged and wear bathing suits and still be Christians.—*Kansas City Star*, 28 June 1931

Indeed, all colonists appeared as children to outsiders, who condescended to their inexperience with modern society:

Barlow said that in spite of the fact that these people had spent their whole lives without a unit of measuring work, they now are responding to the whistle, punching the time-clock, and checking off hours in the field with a fine spirit of cooperation.

The habit of exchanging money, which has become so common to most Americans, was something which required time for the Amanas. Older people left the stores fondling their change and trying to become accustomed to the feel of it.—*Cedar Rapids Gazette*, 20 July 1932

It took a depression and a revolution by ballot to put these infants-in-self-support on the payroll. — *Philadelphia Record,* 18 June 1933

Now, as with Adam and Eve before, each would "earn his bread by the sweat of his face:"

"The chief weakness which led to abandonment of the old communistic system in favor of the present capitalistic setup was the failure on the part of too many members of the society to accept individual responsibilities and obligations in relating to the whole group," says Arthur Barlow, business manager of the society. "This weakness was due largely to a lack of incentive opportunities to work harder and to develop latent abilities, especially on the part of the younger members.

"The capitalistic system, combined with certain benefits, offering the much needed opportunities brought immediate response. Imaginations were fired and ambitions were stimulated; in fact, a new era of expanding life was entered into."— *Kansas City Star,* 7 November 1943

Curiously, few articles reflect on the religious significance of the Change. One, filled with inaccuracies regarding the social structure and religious culture of the community, first appeared in *Christian Century* and was later excerpted in the *Des Moines Record.* The article argued that the "real Amana" had not been transformed as the other articles all suggested but rather had been thoroughly destroyed, replaced by "just another set-up of 'modified capitalism'":

And as is generally the case, its corruption is attributed to an outside influence while a remedy is sought in economic formulae and experimentation. It will, no doubt, never occur to Amana that it should go back to the devotion of its founders, for neither does it occur to us that we might reclaim the animation of seemingly outmoded institutions. — *Des Moines Register,* 1 September 1932

The Society chose to reply to this criticism from the outside. In a letter to the editor of *Christian Century,* the Society's secretary voiced its objections to "certain untruths contained in article entitled, 'Amana—the Glory Has Departed'":

In the first place, it voiced an opinion derogatory to the reorganization of our society, implying that the change made was a mercenary or greedy one which was not at all the case. The change was brought about through inherent defects in communism such as inefficiency of communistic labor, lack of the spirit of sacrifice . . . and economic pressure due to the depression, financial losses, and the ever increasing burden of taxation. The change was made very reluctantly and with the aim of retaining and carrying out the purposes of the old corporation as far as possible.[9]

The letter went on to correct both specific errors, such as the statement that the old society had never paid taxes, and general impressions—insisting, for example, that not only were the Amana people themselves nonmercenary, but so too was Barlow, who acted "completely in harmony with the religious and benevolent character of the society."[10] Thus the new corporate leadership was quick to pick up the old trustees' role of maintaining proper relations with the outside world, including answering criticism whenever it appeared.

In any case the implied criticism of a loss of devotion was definitely the minority view. Most papers tipped their hats to the religious past but generously approved of the colonists' taking "a practical view" of the situation at last. For their typically American fable the journalists found a typically upbeat ending. Hard work would carry the Amanas through the Depression, rewarding them at the end with all the fruits of modernity. Electrification—symbol of modern life—would create a new paradise:

Modern Conveniences

Hausfrau and fraulein beaming over power laundry equipment, joyous with new conveniences and comforts in the living room, kitchen and bath room. Furnishings replaced, remade—even one old sedate grandfather clock, in the Fred Schneider home at West Amana, converted from solemn tick-tock to electric hum.

Grossmutter with her well worn Bible beside a reading lamp. Father with suppressed glee going from switch to switch, a boy again with a new toy, a toy that leaps startlingly from ornate fixtures.

Electric Train

Kinder in wide-eyed wonder scooting whistling trains through tunnels and past semaphores. One lad, Billy Noe, son of John Noe at Amana, weeks ago, soon after Saint Nicholas had come and gone, built his track, station, bridges, and stockyard, awaiting the impulse of electric energy. When the juice was switched on a few days ago, the engine whistled and away it went pulling its load. Since that time Billy loathes taking time out for meals or slumber, to say nothing of school.

A second Christmas for Billy. A second Christmas for the entire community, young and old.

The Society of True Inspiration never will be the same again.—*Cedar Rapids Gazette*, 7 March 1937

The story thus starts in Eden and ends with Christmas. In its telling the national press succeeded in doubly mythologizing Amana. By eulogizing religious devotion and praising capitalist endeavor, the press created a myth that in the end had more to do with mainstream American concerns than with colony history.

POSTSCRIPT TO THE CREATION OF A MYTH

The story, in truth, does not end there. By the date of this last article, 1937, the economic and social transformation of the Amanas was essentially accomplished, with the communards now stockholders, their homes electrified and bright. The fact of the Amana Change had not just entered history but had become myth, a story that could henceforward be pulled out of newspaper files and revived to serve its purpose—to remind a people who they were and what they believed. In 1946, for example, *American Magazine* published an article entitled "Communism Goes Broke in Iowa," which contrasted the failures of the old system with the successes of the new:

In 1946, it is estimated, the Amana Society will produce crops, livestock, and manufactured goods worth $6,000,000. In 1928 and 1929, banner years in American business, with the same acreage of land, the same natural resources, and a population only one sixth smaller, Amana's production was valued at $600,000 annually—one-tenth of the current figure.

What accounts for this vast increase in production? One thing and one thing only: an outright shift from communism to capitalism.[11]

Once again, as in 1932, Amana was seen as "the ideal setup for communism," a group held together by faith instead of coercion, a utopian commune characterized by discipline and with "no unconventional sexual notions with which other communist groups upset their neighbors." Once again it was the "young, realistic members" who most clearly saw the need for change and, as the article continued, "the results are too clear to argue with":

An organization doing a mediocre business under a finespun academic theory has been transformed into a vital, high-powered American corporation through which individual enterprise and the profit motive have produced stupendous financial and social achievements. . . .

Everywhere in Amana one finds enthusiasm for the present system. Why? I asked everywhere. The reasons were characteristically American. A man gets what he earns—no more, no less. The people live better. They get more and sounder education. They have more freedom for individual expression. The family—not the community as in communist times—has become the real unit of life. Amana feels itself an integral part of America.

Old Adolf Heinemann, who complained of waste years ago, finds his views justified by the new capitalist system. "Under communism," he said to me "I saw food wasted, I saw labor wasted, I saw the smartness of our young people wasted. I wish we had been smart enough to adopt capitalism when I was a boy. It works, my good friend, it works." [12]

They did indeed seem to have taken a "practical view of things," and their pragmatism appeared to be paying off. Conservative publications like *American Magazine* found in Amana's continuing success story proof of the superiority of American life: values were proved by appeal not to principle but to productivity: "It works, my good friend, it works."

Throughout the cold war decade of the fifties Amana continued to be used as evidence for the superiority of American capitalism. In 1961, in a speech presented to the American Association for State and Local History, an Amana spokesman told how on the popular Dave Garroway television program, recorded during the time of Khrushchev's visit to Des Moines, Garroway had asked the Amana representative to compare the old Amana with the new Russia:

I said that the Amana type of communism, in its birth, in its intent, and in its implementation, was as far away from the Russian political communism as the village of Amana is from Moscow. In fact, communism as we know it today, in its meaning and application, did not exist in Amana. The communal ownership of the property was really an expedient used to solve an economic problem rather than a basic doctrine as part of the faith. [13]

Year after year and continuing into the present, journalists and writers have trekked out to Amana. Amana is good material for them—not simply for its dramatic historical development and for the local color it provides, but also because of its value as myth, because of the extent to which we as Americans look to it to see ourselves. But before we gaze too long at the reflection, we must return to the history that inspired it. Clearly, in voting for the Change the Amana people had once again, as when they first gathered on the German estates, then emigrated to America, then, critically, developed their communal structure and relocated in Iowa, chosen a strategy that would allow their survival as a community. What alterations followed, how Amana residents renegotiated their compact with American society, are the topics that concern us in the chapters that follow.

PART III

Post-Change Social Life

$\mathbb{A}$MANA Society *Bulletin* notice, 2 June 1932: "Some people still seem to be under the wrong impression that corporation property is everybody's property and can be taken at will. We wish to make it clear that this is not so. Proper steps will have to be taken in the future to avoid further misappropriations."

THE REASSERTION OF AUTHORITY

The changeover from communalism to capitalism did indeed demand considerable psychic and economic adjustment both by individual residents and by community organizations. Through the Change, the economic organization of the Amanas had been stood on its head, with private profit taking over from communal sharing as the organizing principle. Under the direction of Barlow and the new trustees, the Amana Society instituted changes to render their enterprises more efficient and more profitable—including, as we have seen, forcing out many small craft shops and starting major new businesses. Ten short years after the Change, the new corporation could boast of a new woolen mill salesroom, two sandwich shops, a feed department, a new building and repair department, an insurance division, a refrigeration department, and the consolidation of the former village bakeries at South Amana. Other services were quickly established, with two gasoline service stations operating by November 1932, the

Amana Society Service Company for electricity established in 1932, and the Amana Society Telephone Company founded in 1941.[1] Amana had moved quickly to stabilize her new economic basis.

The political role of the corporation was more difficult to determine. Early in the post-Change days, the Amana Society tried to convince the membership that Society directors now exercised the same moral power as had been held by the elders. *Bulletin* announcements reflect corporation attempts to regulate both the economic and the political affairs of the community. The 2 June 1932 *Bulletin*, for example, still largely devoted to establishing economic guidelines ("Bread will be regarded as fresh for a period of not less than 24 hours after baking," "Apiaries were disposed of to the highest bidders"), included the hands-off warning regarding corporate property quoted above. But the problem apparently continued, so that the 3 August 1933 *Bulletin* carried the following resolution:

BE IT RESOLVED that any member unlawfully taking Corporation property or any member making false statements about those in authority or spreading misinformation about the Society's business, shall be punished in accordance with the laws and statutes of this county and the Amana Society.

Furthermore, anyone taking Corporation property unlawfully or making false statements or spreading misinformation will naturally have a black mark against him in the matter of employment, compensation, etc.

The final sentence reflects the fact that the Society's real power lay in its controlling hold over the Amana economy. Religious myth no longer legitimated this power, however, so resort to the courts was occasionally necessary, as demonstrated by a 1933 larceny case in which a member was accused of stealing corporation property.

In other instances the Society's attempt to "play elder" through controlling social behavior quite apart from its economic interest was more obvious, if less successful. The 10 August 1933 *Bulletin*, for example, instructed residents to "Please take notice that gas station attendants at Amana are required to turn names in to the Main Office of any one loafing about pumps or driveways," and the 24 August issue noted that:

Our young folks should take warning not to obstruct the public highway at street corners in the villages or otherwise. This is especially dangerous at night when crowds assemble and cars are being parked, sometimes even without parking lights. Accidents could easily happen this way and bring you and other people in trouble.

After 1933 these notices subside somewhat (although throughout the years dog owners continue to be warned to keep their pets out of other people's flowerbeds), which suggests both that residents settled into their new work and consumption roles and also that the Society itself came to realize that adequate control lay in its ability to determine economic rewards.

SOCIAL LIFE

Along with these new economic roles, residents were adapting to new patterns of socializing. Increasingly, extracommunity social networks were layered on top of family and village-based ties as the culture of modern society itself, with its own values and organizations, developed on top of the still rural and Germanic base of the old Amana. It often happens that when close community ties are weakened or destroyed social clubs form to fill the gap.[2] In Amana this was doubly the case as colonists, often acting through a sense of inferiority vis-à-vis the outside, rushed to prove their membership in the dominant society. Yet in reading through the weekly *Bulletins* published between 1932 and 1959, one is struck not just by the adoption of social forms, essentially complete by the mid-1950s, but also by the sporadically surfacing fear of losing the characteristics that made Amana distinctive. How this sense of loss was translated into action and itself became a new rallying point for sociability will be treated later on. Here the focus is on how the values and forms of sociability characteristic of modern American society completed their invasion of Amana, an invasion started long before the Change itself. The actual transition can be broken into three subperiods: the 1930s, years of tension between community and society values and structures; the war years, when Amana proved its 100 percent American status; and the postwar years, when a validated Amana joined the rest of America in a celebration of democracy and family and the comforts of modernity.

THE THIRTIES

In 1932, even with the long-announced Change completed, the colonists were newcomers to consumerism. The first year's *Bulletins* are largely concerned with economic problems, but by 1933 there are already signs of growing links with the outside. The *Chicago Herald* is now available at the Amana gas station, and outside visitors are increasingly common at the now-legal baseball games. There are still lessons to be learned, however. Residents and store owners are told to pick up the phone right away when it rings—"It is customary everywhere that phone calls are given precedence over all other business"—and, also in 1933, the first of many warnings is given against driving cars too fast over the narrow and dusty roads. Some debate takes place regarding whether all social practices of the greater society should find a welcome in Amana. One article critical of social dancing asks, "What would the outside world think?"[3]

TRADITIONS

Here is a call to you young folk who are so full of life and eagerness to get your full share of pleasure—should we cause needless pain? . . . For this reason we should avoid such forms of amusements as for instance public dancing, which jar too much the old principles and especially the traditions of the Church. . . . Furthermore, what would the outside world think of us if we were not willing to uphold now under the new regime that which Amana stood for in the past, namely a sane, conservative view in regard to any changes that have to be brought about, without too much radical plunging into new channels. Is it not much better to comply with the wishes of the older people and the traditions of the Society and thereby make it unnecessary for the Corporation to prohibit, as you no doubt well appreciate that the Corporation has control of its property and the purposes for which it may be used.

Social dancing may be frowned upon, but the next year the Boy Scouts and Girls Club are organized, a beauty shop is opened, and Bill Zuber, so fond of pitching onions behind the barns, is off on the start of his major-league career. The first all-colony club is founded in 1933, and, as author resident Rettig describes it:

Calling itself the Amana Community Club, it generated the aura of an embryo country club with its tennis matches, bowling alley, billiard table, auditorium, and reading rooms. It also planned to sponsor educational and recreational projects on a community-wide basis. The approximately fifty members included bakers, butchers, carpenters, cabinetmakers, farmers, salesmen, officemen, teachers, pharmacists, dentists, and doctors from the seven colonies.[4]

Electrification comes to Amana in 1937, about the same time as to other rural areas, and a good number of the traditional old grandfather clocks are turned electric.[5] Announcements increase in the latter 1930s of new Chevys and Ford V-eights. Yet farm news is also still big news. The village of Amana reports one week that "One of the horses died this week of lung hemorrhage. It was only eight years old," and the village of Homestead reports having sold Toby the bull to East Amana. Some members express fears that Amana is moving away from the use of German—"an inheritance of great value"—while others come to accept baseball and social dancing in principle ("two of the most noted physical culture exercises endorsed by leading authorities") if not always in practice ("Both of these exercises, however, have to be done in the right way, especially the latter: otherwise it is detrimental to sociability and interfering with the laws of religion"). In addition, social notes (who visits whom, celebrates or acquires what) gain in popularity through the decade. Thus, whereas in 1934 the *Bulletin* correspondent complains of newsmakers who object, "No, oh no, don't put that in the Bulletin," by 1938 the notices are so popular and extensive that the correspondent can delight in describing the *Bulletin* as "a flower garden in which the good-natured readers and contributors are classed as flowers which give their fragrance to the enjoyment of others."

THE FORTIES

By the 1940s many of these tensions between old and new social forms have been resolved. Social clubs continue to proliferate: the Young Men's Bureau is organized, as are several 4-H clubs. The junior class at the high school presents *Cupid at Vassar*, and moviegoers thrill to *Gaucho Serenade* at the clubhouse. But Amana social life in the early 1940s is colored by America's entrance into World War II. The community's former pietism had earlier forbidden taking oaths and entering into military combat, and the community suffered abuse and insult from neighbors for its pacifist stance in World War I.[6] In World War II Amana leaves the question up to the individual, and the 22 December 1939 *Bulletin* can proudly report that "only two persons in our town and a few in towns across the Iowa River have registered as non-combatants."[7] Red Cross knitters organize and start their industrious clicking. Soon the *Bulletin* is filled with reports of Amana servicemen, and occasionally of an Amana son killed in combat. The refrigeration department steps up production. All this activity stemmed in part from sheer patriotism, in part from past pacifism, in part from fear that, as a German colony, they would be associated with the enemy. Of course, it was also good business. The *Bulletin* carefully informs its readers in January 1942 of the Alien Registration Act:

The President of the United States has . . . directed in the interests of national safety that alien enemies should not possess or use radio transmitting sets, short wave radio receiving sets, cameras, firearms, and ammunitions. In order to carry out these regulations effectively it is necessary to require alien enemies to deposit such prohibited articles in law enforcement agencies. . . . It is noted that aliens in this country are Japanese, German, and Italian aliens.

The notice is repeated the following week with the comment, "It is realized that probably all enemy aliens . . . in this area are law abiding citizens and Sheriff Engelbert was instructed to arrange for them to deposit these articles with as little inconvenience as possible." That same week Abbott and Costello appear in *Keep 'Em Flying* at the clubhouse, and one of innumerable war poems sees print: "Lord, make a mighty SOLDIER of my son! / To wage the war of life till he has won!"

By the war's end Amana had proved its patriotism through its soldiers, its league of women knitters, and a special government award won by the refrigeration plant for its wartime effort. Amana residents could now settle down to the good life. Mid-1940s *Bulletin*s are filled with wedding announcements describing sumptuous affairs a far cry from the austere ceremonies of old. The baby boom follows in Amana as elsewhere, with newborns being given such un-Amanalike names as "Tamara Lynn" and "Wade Daniel." Houses are constructed for returning GI's, and the largest development is soon labeled "Boystown." In 1948 the presidential train passes through town (the *Bulletin* comment: "Frankly, it was quite an ordinary looking train").

Reflecting attitudes and concerns of the late 1940s, at a Y-Teen conference in 1949 Amana representatives attend discussions on topics such as "What is Russia up to?" "Why are people prejudiced?" and "How may I get along better with the people around me?"

THE FIFTIES

The fifties, known now as an age of cold war and prosperity, had their reflection in the Amanas. Amana people felt more secure than ever in their choices: any reference in tourist brochures to the old order made it clear that Amana *communalism* was not to be confused with Russian *communism*. In 1954 four Amana men are honored to attend a Republican dinner at which Vice-President Nixon is the invited speaker. The two-tone automobile becomes the fifties status symbol, especially in a community where houses are relatively similar despite attempts at individualistic touches. One man makes an impression in his two-tone chartreuse Chevrolet; another tops that with an ivory-and-orange Plymouth. In the social notes, visits of Amana people to each other's homes are crowded out by more exciting visitors: a Ghanaian student invited to dinner, a roller-skating party held to raise funds for a Navaho boy, visits to and from relatives scattered across the United States.

Thus, by the time of its 1959 centennial celebration of the completed move to Iowa Amana had effected a layering of cultures wherein the social forms of modern society structured the activities of residents still attached in varying degrees to the forms of old. The same *Bulletin* that reported the participation in the centennial of the prince and princess of Ysenberg-Budingen, descendants of the prince who had once sheltered the Inspirationists, also announced that the refrigeration plant had become one of the ten largest factories in the Cedar Rapids area and that its products were being sold in every state and in fifty-six foreign countries. Truly, the isolation the group originally sought on the German estates seemed to have completely disappeared.

And yet, even as residents enjoyed their modern life and its appurtenances, they were expressing concern over just what this integration symbolized for them and their community. Starting in the 1950s though gathering substantial momentum only in the 1970s, they found one way to maintain both tradition and a sense of special status through a return to the past, not in actuality but as history.

Faith in the New Amana

CHAPTER 12

Fᴏʀ many who live in the villages today, religion is still the heartbeat of the Amanas. Every Sunday residents can be seen quietly entering the plain, steepleless churches, men in coats and ties, the women more traditional with their small black caps, shawls, and aprons worn over their modern dresses. As in earlier days the men enter through their door, the women through theirs, and take their places, no longer strictly assigned by age and merit, on opposite sides of the church. However, it does not seem to be chance alone that leads the older women to arrive early and claim the back benches, which used to carry the highest status. They apparently feel they have earned the right to these positions and the excellent view they afford of the whole congregation.

CHURCH STRUCTURE

In a changing society, the church has altered somewhat in function. With the secular branch of the reorganized community, the Amana Society, now serving the controlling function the church formerly fulfilled, the church is freed to play a highly symbolic role, to serve as an affective rallying point for community members, who can now worship as their grandparents did without suffering the same daily restraints.[1] Under the reorganization, the church was kept intact as far as was believed possible, partly to appease those members who distrusted any change whatever in the community. In the new church constitution, leadership was granted to thirteen trustees, to be elected by church members from among the existing elders. These trustees tend to hold office until retirement or death. Since the Change there have been only two church board presidents. Under the new constitution the church can punish or expel members, and it maintains control over all church property, including church buildings and cemeteries. Since the Amana schools (now part of the public school system) can no longer teach religion, Sunday schools were established in 1933.[2]

The frequency and schedule of the church meetings has changed as well. After the Change evening prayer and all daytime services during the week were gradually discontinued. Now only Sunday morning services are held, along with special services on the evening of New Year's Day, during Holy Week, and on Thanksgiving, Christmas, and New Year's Eve. The *Bundesschliessung*, a special service signifying the renewal of the covenant among members, is still observed at the Thanksgiving service, as it has been since 1866. The dreaded *Unterredung* has been replaced by a much milder form of repentance service, the *Bussversammlung*, at which no public confession is required. The *Liebesmahl*, that more joyful special occasion, was first discontinued, then reinstated in 1956.[3] No longer are there congregations segregated by age: today all adults participate either in the German service or in the English service that was initiated in 1960.

In the German services much of the old has remained. The several elders take their turns presiding over the services, which begin with a hymn from the *Psalterspiel*, a book of mostly old German verses without printed music, sung a cappella. A *Werkzeug* testimony selected by the elder is read, then the congregation and elders kneel facing their benches. In the German services all may recite personal prayers in turn, a practice omitted in the English service, which moves directly to a member's recitation of the Apostles' Creed. A general prayer is then offered by the presiding elder, followed by the Lord's Prayer recited by the congregation. A passage from the Bible is read, and then the elder presents a short sermon. In earlier years this was followed by supportive comments from the elders, but this practice has now been discarded in both services. Finally there is another hymn; in the English service the last verse is sung standing. Then the benediction is spoken, any announcements are made, and the congregation files out row by row.[4]

A visitor would note certain differences between these church gatherings and those of other congregations. Many members arrive early, as much as half an hour. No one arrives late; anyone who has the misfortune to do so will be the focus of attention. There is little talking before or after the service. A few words may be passed, but there is not the socializing commonly associated with Sunday services. Also this is the one part of their life that residents strongly do not want photographed or in any other way interfered with by tourists. A devout church member who otherwise is welcoming toward visitors complained one Sunday:

> I don't mind if they come to worship with us, that's different. But when they come into church, whole busloads full, and in jeans or pant suits and the men in shirt sleeves. They often don't keep quiet either, the kids rustle the papers and you know how silent the service should be. You're used to looking ahead of you and seeing your friends on the benches and instead you see tourists. I don't care what else they do, just leave us our church.

Particularly welcome, though, are visitors from other practicing religious groups, such as the Mennonites, whom the people of Amana regard warmly as coreligionists, at least in the historical sense.[5]

Other changes demonstrate a renewed interest in the church, at least by some members. A number of people have translated testimonies as well as hymns, and one has assumed the even greater task of translating the volumes of the *Inspirations-Historie*. As she explained the basis of her interest:

> A couple of summers ago special church meetings were held on Sunday evenings for two or three hours to explain the Amana religion. That's how I became interested. G—— asked me to do a sketch of all the *Werkzeuge*. I started, became very interested, and did the presentation, which lasted two sessions. At these church meetings I kept saying "Someone should translate the *Inspirations-Historie*." I kept saying, "They should do it" and then I began to wonder, "Who is this mystical person?" So I started in November 1975. Now I'm up to 1817 and the Reawakening and working on the index to the second volume.

Another significant change is the invitation extended to women to lead services. Although Landmann was a *Werkzeug*, neither she nor any other woman has held the position of elder.[6] Two women have led services, though not as elders, and their inclusion seemed to stir little controversy.[7]

The invitation to Amana women to become elders reflects the trend in other denominations to open the ministry to women and also, possibly, the rising status of women. Yet in Amana, as on the outside, given the increasing difficulty of recruiting men into the ministry, the acceptance of women may indicate not just overdue recognition of women's capabilities but also the declining power and significance of the church. Elders still have status, but they retain little of their former power. Eldership is still an honor, yet with today's busy tempo it may seem more a time-consuming burden and less a sacred communal trust.

PROBLEMS AFFECTING THE AMANA CHURCH

Although the church structure has thus changed and adapted over time, two problems have continued to plague it. The first is the size and attitude of the membership, the second the strength and depth of the leadership. After the Change as before, the "lukewarm" attitude of many members toward their church was deplored. In May 1934 the Amana Society *Bulletin* carried an article by an elder stressing that, while the business aspect of the reorganized community seemed strong despite the Depression, the church needed "a similar revival." "A church organization, the same as any other organization, is not stronger than the members comprising it. A lukewarm attitude and half-hearted cooperation makes a weak organization."[8]

Such warnings, however, had little effect. Perhaps the lowest point in church history occurred in the late 1950s. By that time many of the younger people were no longer fluent in the German language, and even some elders found it difficult to conduct the whole service in German. Despite some opposition, in 1960 it was finally decided that English services would be instituted; that decision was probably one of the key reasons for a revival of interest. Some older residents resent services' being held in English, saying, "I like to hear it in German." They can, of course, for one German congregation meets every Sunday. It is rather that the use of English represents for them an offense against a cherished tradition; possibly also they sense a loss of mystery and group distinction.[9]

Some younger members, however, were demanding even greater changes—specifically, the discontinuation of the women's distinctive church costume. This suggestion was firmly rejected by the church leaders, as in the following statement from the "Church News" column of the *Bulletin*:

It has been stated that these English services are a new venture and that they are meant as an addition to our regular German services. A group of young men have volunteered to help the good cause along by accepting "elderships" with some none-too-easy duties. Do you want to support them and help this cause along too? Then the women members of the Church Society who are attending these services should wear their usual church garb—cap, apron and *Halstuch* please. It was mutually agreed that certain things would remain the same as in years gone by and that Amana's heritage would remain evident not only in our style of service but also in the dress pattern of the *Schwestern* in church. . . .

Whenever different nationalities, such as the Swiss, or Spanish or Swedish, meet at any of their own important festivities, they proudly wear their so-called national garb for the occasion. They know that on that day they are dressed differently and in an ancient fashion all their own, but it means something to them to be recognized as descendants of some fine people. Amana too is different and its faith has chosen to "remain true" and to stay that way. . . .

Dressing alike for regular church services by women members and their teen-aged daughters is helpful so that silks and satins of many styles and furs and fabrics do not distract from the simplicity which the Amana faith tries to maintain and support in its services. Anyone who loves his or her church to that extent can only be respected for such devotion.[10]

Besides the problem of maintaining the enthusiasm of its members, the church has reason for concern about the declining number of elders. The decline itself dates from the 1880s and the death of the last *Werkzeug*, but the loss is increasingly serious, and several churches have closed owing to lack of elders. The peak of ninety-one elders in the period 1884–1907 declined to sixty-four for 1908–31, which further declined in the postwar era (1932–51), when there were only thirty-four elders. Between

1952 and 1970 the community lost another five, so that the number of elders totaled only twenty-nine.[11] At present fifteen elders lead the German and English services. There are no elders for the villages of West and East Amana, and High Amana has been left with one. Services have been consolidated so that the residents of the seven villages, who under the old communal system worshipped in their separate village churches, now join together to worship at either the German service or the English service.

These difficulties result in part from the increasing number of outsiders living within the Amanas. Such newcomers may move in, but they worship out. The action in 1960 to provide English services was seen as one means of assuring that both outsiders who had moved or married into the Amanas, along with younger residents of old Amana stock, would be more likely to attend services than if they were left with the old German format they could hardly understand. This maneuver was somewhat successful in increasing attendance and interest in church, yet today many complain that members of insider/outsider marriages, as well as some insiders themselves, worship at mainstream Protestant churches in Williamsburg, Cedar Rapids, or Marengo.

Because of these problems, the existing elders find themselves involved in what one termed a "recruiting effort." As one elder described the situation:

There is a hesitancy of young people to take on an eldership. It either interferes with their private lives or they don't feel they have the necessary qualifications. You have to leave it up to the individual. When you talk or speak to them they tell you that they don't have the qualifications. It's a feeling we all have. You feel terribly alone when you sit there by yourself. We have 130, 150 people here at the service in Amana. . . . Almost all of those people who have been approached should realize that this is something they have to cope with and overcome. I'll say this, if we don't get the elders we need, we *will* reach the crisis point in about five years.

While most elders tend to express confidence in their church— "It was there before I was born, it will be there after I die"— many church members are less hopeful about its future and can consider the day when someone—a minister from the outside or even someone from inside the Amanas—will be paid to function in the capacity formerly assumed as a position of honor and power. Indeed, it was reported that one man who was approached did raise the question of monetary compensation. The loss of the *Werkzeuge* a century ago signaled a critical decline for the church; is the declining number of elders today signaling its demise?

The early pietists, the Inspirationists among them, attempted to forge links between religious thought and the structure of daily life: every personal act was thought to assume public and religious significance. Pietism stressed the necessity of revolutionizing social structures and people's lives to bring them more in accord with biblical direction and belief. Certainly such a radical interpretation of religion's task is a far cry from the "no offense" brand of Christianity many see as currently dominant in our society, one that seems to soften the edges of competing theologies.[12] Within the Amanas much of the pietist message has been watered down over time, though Amana residents who speak of their faith surprise outsiders unable to understand belief in so small, so "irrational," a church. But with the fading of active inspiration, with the limitations placed on the number and form of the services, with the difficulties of maintaining a volunteer eldership or even Sunday morning attendance—but most important with the 1932 redefinition of the community's basis from the sacred to the secular—the Amanas are blending in with the mainstream of American religious thought and practice.

While in Amana the pietist message was eventually diluted and made more easily digestible, in other ways pietism as a religious force has maintained its radical thrust:

The pietist communards were among those . . . who look to a God who keeps his promises, who is not content to let his creation decline and collapse at the hands of wicked men in high places, who proposes a restoration of all things to their original perfection. The communes they founded were "Schools of Christ," within which men and women were readying themselves for the Kingdom of God which was at hand. In this setting, they were not only avid students of history; they were responsible protagonists.[13]

Pietism specifically—and more generally all impulse toward theocracy—appears as a two-edged sword, leading alternatively toward humanity and inhumanity, toward charity and oppres-

sion. When it is located safely in the past, it is easy to romanti-
cize. In the present, however, the threats implicit in religious
control over institutions and activities are more apparent: while
Jonestown was not a pietist experiment by any means, the possibility of such autocratic control remains. On the other side of
the sword lies the dream of human perfectibility. Today some still
opt for the dream: witness the proliferation of cults exerting
more control over their members than the *Werkzeuge* ever imag-
ined possible. The majority, however, are more likely to predict
disaster. Many might agree with Conor Cruise O'Brien that "the
thought of the capacity of spiritual power to alter material relations in the world should be sobering rather than reassuring." [14]
To some extent we have moved in this nation from a myth based
primarily on religious interpretation to one reflecting a different
set of values and orientations. The Inspirationist church continues, but its hold today is distinctly more powerful over hearts
than over minds.

New Economic Structures

T_{ODAY} the corporation dominates the local economic scene, and to some extent the Amanas resemble a company town. The Society, however, now a modern and highly diversified collection of businesses, still finds cause to call upon the past religious myth to legitimate its present capitalist endeavors. In the annual report for 1977 the president stressed the spirit of the old communal society continuing in the new corporation:

Once again let us be reminded of the fortitudes and willingness of our forefathers to undergo hardships and sacrifice and that they based their decisions on integrity and honesty and never shirked an honest responsibility, but rather sought only that which was right and prudent according to their unwavering faith in God! It was they who gave us something to cherish and perpetuate. Likewise let us not falter but strive honestly and sincerely to remain worthy of the trust and responsibility that they have placed in us. May the name "Amana" inspire us to greater efforts in whatever our task or our part in the overall effort for the year may be. Let it always be a challenge to us never to be complacent but always to strive for perfection and self-satisfaction in what we are accomplishing.

This appeal to tradition should not hide the fact that the Amana Society is a powerful corporation with numerous operations, from the small village stores to the woolen mill and the furniture manufacturing shop.

With such extensive operations, the Amana Society is a major employer in the community. The consolidation of village farms into one major division, along with other streamlining effects and modern improvements in farming, has resulted in a decline in employees in this, the major money-making operation of the Society. Meanwhile, the building of the "Little Amana" tourist complex on Route 80 has provided new job opportunities for Amana and area residents.

Changes have also occurred in the numbers and privileges of stockholders, changes that have threatened the equality implicit in the changeover plans. By the 1950s certain problems had become evident in the regulation and distribution of stock, including the rising value of class A stocks, which made it prohibitive for young people to buy into the Amana Society, the expense to the corporation of free medical and dental care, and specific management problems, including the extent to which outside experts should be used in deciding Society matters. Disagreement over these issues led to a lawsuit and further lengthy legal proceedings that dominated the decade 1955–65 and were resolved only in 1972, with the stockholders' acceptance of a revised plan. Under this plan the old class A stock was split into a new type at the ratio of one old share to one hundred new shares, and the new shares no longer carried free medical care and burial. Thus the "one man/one vote" principle carried over from the old system finally had to be discarded to allow new purchasers into the body of stockholders, while the Society's obligation to pay medical expenses (again a carryover from the church's role of caring for its members) was phased out so that the Society could concentrate on its major goals. It was slowly being forced to abjure the principles of equality and security it had worked so long to protect.[1]

The Amana Society has thus inherited from the old board of trustees the role of major decision-making power, insofar as the Amanas, as an unincorporated area, lack any separate local municipal government. Thus in part by default the corporation's control extends to noncorporate matters, usually handled by municipal authorities. Members of its board of directors themselves are somewhat divided on the Amana Society's exact role in the seven villages. As some of them commented:

We're strictly a business corporation. So far as the stockholders are concerned, we're out to make money; we have no other purpose. In this business we have to act in the best interest of stockholders.

We do have a little role in acting as a town government, a municipality. I don't think it's good for us to act this role. It's really an open stock
company now—we can no longer represent everyone equally.

Like it or not, the Amana Society is the city council, getting quite involved in matters and responsibilities that would be in the matter of the
city council and mayor. We have to handle not just the responsibilities of
a corporation, but also neighborly quarrels and decisions.

From the time of the Change, the Amana Society has had to
deal with some problems usually handled by city hall. The
Amana Society Service Company, one of its subdivisions, sup-
plies electricity, water, and telephone service, and a separate
Amana sanitary district was founded, as was an Amana fire district.[2] Law enforcement was long neglected, but in 1977 a security guard was hired, supposedly just to look after Amana Society businesses, but with the unwritten assumption that he
would also check on private businesses. Even with these moves
to divest itself of municipal responsibilities, however, the Amana
Society still exerts extensive control, a control that, we shall see,
is at present being challenged both by private businesses and by
a changing population.

AMANA REFRIGERATION

The Society is not, however, the only game in town. Besides the
corporation—in fact, just down the road from its headquarters—
lies the refrigeration plant. Located on the former woolen mill
site at Middle Amana, the plant, covering twenty-five square acres
plus surrounding grounds, provides employment for twenty-two
hundred workers drawn from Amana and more than one hundred surrounding communities. Encouraged by his initial success at selling beer coolers in the early 1930s, Foerstner and eight
employees began building and selling refrigeration units. The
Amana Society bought out the small business, naming Foerstner
manager and Harry Wendler salesman. The plant was relocated
for a short time at Main Amana, then moved to its present site at
Middle Amana. In 1943 the company suffered a disastrous fire,
with a loss of $225,000, but it soon recovered its economic health,
so that by 1947 it was able to add to its line the upright home

freezer, in 1949 the top freezer/refrigerator combination, then shortly after the side-by-side freezer/refrigerator.[3]

In 1950 the refrigeration company was sold to a group of Cedar Rapids businessmen, with Foerstner remaining on as general manager. In 1965 the company merged with the powerful Raytheon Company, Lexington, Massachusetts, and Foerstner was named president of Amana Refrigeration. A second plant was built in 1968 at Fayetteville, Tennessee, to produce air conditioners, dehumidifiers, furnaces, and trash compactors, and in 1967 the company introduced the first countertop microwave ovens available to the public.[4]

Much like the Amana Society, the refrigeration company gently refers back to the Amana communal and religious past in its slogan—"in the tradition of fine craftsmanship"—and in its advertising. A major campaign running in popular magazines in late 1980 included one advertisement featuring a Smoothtop range in the color photograph's foreground, barns and silos in the distant background (not, in fact, Amana barns). A second advertisement showed a well-stocked refrigerator (broiled lobster, shrimp canapés) backed by the lily lake and accompanied by the following copy:

Wastefulness.
The folks who settled Amana, Iowa, loathed it. So do the folks who build refrigerators today.
So it didn't surprise them any when U.S. Government figures proved that Amana refrigerators have the lowest estimated yearly operating costs in five different size categories.

When tours were still being led through the plant, tour guides emphasized the link to the crafts heritage by pointing out that every refrigerator that passes down the line is given a thorough check and that the Amana microwave ovens are the only brand not required by federal law to carry a warning on their doors. Apart from that, the plant looks like any other industrial plant employing large numbers of people and turning out products for worldwide distribution.

It is somewhat difficult to gauge the company's influence on the community. It provides employment for many within the Amanas and in the surrounding area, and it may encourage Amana's young people to stay in their hometown. The plant contributes indirectly through sponsoring a scholarship fund for children of employees and also a major pro/amateur golf tournament held yearly that attracts many top-ranked professional golfers as well as politicians and celebrities. Although the largest industry and a major taxpayer, Amana Refrigeration appears to maintain a relatively low profile in political and economic matters at the county level. Within Amana, its role in local affairs is nonetheless the subject of considerable speculation and gossip. According to some residents the company played more of a role in community affairs before its merger with Raytheon but since then has maintained a low profile.

PRIVATE BUSINESSES

Besides these two major corporations, many private businesses—wineries, gift shops, restaurants—have grown up within the Amanas and are geared toward the tourists. Some of the oldest and best-established businesses are the restaurants, for good food and plenty of it was always one of Amana's attractions. Tourists would ride in from Iowa City or Davenport and, as roads and cars improved, from increasingly greater distances to taste the family-style cooking. The Colony Inn was founded in 1934, the Ox Yoke Inn in 1940, and the third of the major restaurants in Main Amana, the Ronnenburg Inn, in 1950.[5] Other restaurants followed, as did a number of gift shops and wineries. Furniture shops also trade on old skills with a new market value. The Schanz furniture shop, for example, got its start when Norman Schanz, who had been doing repair work in his spare time, got an order from a woman with three sons and one oak desk who wanted copies made for the other sons. The shop now is engaged in both refinishing and reproduction and was chosen several years ago to do the furniture reproduction work at the Old Capitol building in Iowa City.

Such private businesses vary in their relations to the Amana Society. On the one hand are the businesses like the major restaurants that were established long ago, enjoy tremendous success, and are considered "legitimate" by the corporation. On the other hand are many of the smaller businesses of more recent origin, which are often seen by the corporation as being in competition with its own businesses and are sometimes considered exploitative by community residents who deplore the effect of gift shops and wineries on the appearance of their villages. Such tensions within the community reflect unresolved questions of control inherited from pre-Change days. The corporation, operating without a religious myth but trying to legitimate its authority in part through its ties to the past, has had to call upon the courts to defend its control. This is best seen in the rather bizarre 1978 suit in which the corporation sued several of its own stockholders.

THE LAWSUIT

The 1978–79 lawsuit developed out of the Amana Society's right to accept or reject requests to open or extend businesses and out of similar questions related to zoning. In other communities such zoning requests are usually handled by municipal authorities, but in the Amanas the only restrictions on residents are those found in the Amana Society charter and the deeds given to residents after the 1932 breakup. According to the Society's general manager, the Society, after "much soul searching," decided in the mid 1970s to declare a moratorium on issuing permits for visitor-oriented businesses. The move developed out of a "real and genuine concern" among Society board members that continued commercial exploitation might destroy everything that made Amana a unique attraction. Although the moratorium was instituted at a time when there were no permit applications pending, several new businesses did open and in time became the defendants in the lawsuit. These businesses included a gift shop, a winery, and a furniture store, among others. It was a difficult problem for a closely knit community in which so many people are related, friends, and/or neighbors. There were, for example, several cases in which people being sued had relatives who were members of the Amana Society board of directors. In the month before the trial commenced, the general manager of the Amana Society explained the Society's position:

We have going for us the original restrictions and the signed agreements that they would abide by the acts and restrictions of the Amana Society. The law says that the particular statute does not apply if there is reversion of the land to the original owner, but that's not the case here, so it should apply. If that fails we have a second line of defense, which is the contracts these people signed. Our only primary aim is to make certain the stockholders as a group are involved in any venture the Society and the area engages in. We came here as a group, we have worked as a group.

Others echoed his sentiments, fearing that community solidarity would be threatened by the proceedings.

The critical point before the case was heard seemed to revolve around whether the deed restrictions were still in effect. Another Society director had a more negative appraisal of the strength of the Society's case:

They don't want you to get too successful. It stems back to the old days. You might want to become something different. . . . But the *Bruderrath* tells you no, you have to do this. . . . Now the Amana Society has control—they think—over the deeds. They do have a lot of rules and regulations which are their way of doing things. But they don't have the law. Nobody will benefit from this.

The lawsuit trial, heard in Johnson County District Court, Iowa City, in the fall of 1978, represented just the sort of airing of community affairs the residents feared.[6] Defendants included two wineries accused by the Amana Society of selling nonwine items such as sausages, cheese, and beer. The third defendant, a gift shop (and also the owner of the land on which it stood), was accused of operating without a permit. The other defendants of the originally larger group being sued had settled out of court.

Much of the early testimony and the Society's case centered on local land history, the traditional right of first the church, then the corporation, to control land use in the Amanas. The Society general manager read from passages in the plan of reorganization adopted at the time of the Change in which it was stated:

[It] is fitting and proper and the sense of the society that the property remain as nearly as possible in the present form as the home communities of the members and that the members be accorded preferential rights in acquiring the homes therein. . . .

The corporation should endeavor at all times to maintain control of the real estate now held by the present Society and all deeds executed should as nearly as may be, contain reversionary clauses or restrictions to the end that the control of the real estate be maintained in the new corporation.

The Society contended that the control established at the time of the Change had been agreed to by the community then, again in 1952 at the charter's thirty-year renewal, and once again in an amended charter in 1972. The defendants, however, claimed that a 1965 state statute on deed restrictions rendered the Society's restrictions void, and, second, that the Society had been unduly discriminatory in the enforcement of its control. The fact of Amana's status as a National Landmark was also hauled into the legal battle, with the general manager reporting that the colonies would lose both financial and advisory benefits if no controls were exerted over commercial development. In fact, Society concern with just such overcommercialization, the manager claimed, had been behind the 1974 moratorium on further business permits.

While seemingly a purely internal question, the Amana lawsuit thus quickly assumed importance beyond its boundaries. Once again the outside society, this time in the guise of preservationist interests, had a stake in the outcome. The head of the review unit of the National Register of Historic Places was called in to testify and emphasized both the uniqueness of the Amanas and the danger in which they stood. Amana, he reported, was the only one of a dozen utopian societies within the broader category of social and humanistic movements that enjoyed the Landmark designation. Landmarks, the "cream" of historic places, were eligible for fifty-fifty matching federal funds to provide preservation planning, to cover such expenses as installing security systems, to provide limited protection from a decrease in historic value caused by any project receiving federal funding or licensing, and also for tax incentives for preservation. Biennial studies of the colonies, he said, showed "the possibility of trouble in maintaining the Landmark designation because of their popularity and consequent tourist traffic." Thus it was clear that historicity—and dollars—could be withdrawn by federal decision.

Besides the fuzzy issue of the legality of deed restrictions (not renewed by the Society in compliance with the state's stale-use statute), the defendants' counterattack focused on inconsistencies in the application of control. They alleged that other violations existed that were overlooked, and they pointed to one Society director who parked a backhoe and truck that he used for construction on land rented from the Society for twenty-five dollars. Another director was accused by the defendants of renting out tourist rooms. The general manager argued those two charges while admitting that some other cases of retail selling were allowed because they were only occasional and often consisted of elderly people selling handicrafts. The beer room at Die Heimat motel was accepted because it was for motel guests only, the cocktail lounge at the Ronnenburg restaurant had approval because it was part of the restaurant. Gifts could be sold at the High Amana store because this allowed the store to stay open for food purchases by the village's elderly. The defendants also attacked the large number of goods not made in Amana but sold by corporation businesses. The manager answered that as of 1 January 1979 only products made by the Amana Society would bear the Amana trademark: all others would be identified with the phrases "distributed by . . ." or "manufactured by . . ."

When the decision finally came down in late February, five months after the trial began, the judge found for the Society, stating that under the reorganization the Society had assumed right of property control. As for the defendants' argument that, under the stale-use statute, restrictions on record for more than twenty-one years were no longer valid unless updated, the judge argued that, while the Society may have failed to renew the recorded deeds, an "unrecorded collateral agreement" had been proved to exist. The "general understanding that the Society must give consent to types of businesses operating in the Colonies" ensured that no "fast food establishments, motels, movie theatres, nightclubs, bars [or] bowling alleys" would threaten the community's historic character. The judge concluded, "The Society has absolute discretion to determine whether a business can be conducted on land subject to deeds, what the nature of the business can be and how long it can be conducted there." Preservationists were pleased, the Society board was pleased. Residents, however, continued to ask, "But who will control the Society?"

In the ensuing years, however, this question would change to the broader one, "Who will control?" For in 1981 the Iowa Supreme Court reversed the lower court's decision. The argument was that the Society appeared to have no general plan for land development and that other mechanisms of control could be implemented to safeguard the Amana heritage. At public meetings held in Amana in 1982, most people present expressed approval of "some form of democratically administered controls." Alternatives under consideration included county zoning, the creation of historic districts, incorporation as a municipality, and some form of special legislation. The Society itself maintained a low profile in these discussions; research into the viability of the alternatives above was conducted by a committee of residents who were due to report in the fall of 1982 with their recommendation on what path to pursue.

Thus, despite such continuing tensions between individual and community, a transition has been effected from church to corporation, with the authority structure of the old largely duplicated in the new, and this authority is only now being seriously questioned. Perhaps only adoption of this archetypal modern institution—the corporation—could ensure the Amana Colonies' continuation as a coherent community with vital links to its past.[7] Only the corporation could supply an adequate, if flawed, solution to demands for increased individualism, efficiency, and conformity with the modern world. But certain questions remained unanswered, having to do with the uses to which the former communalism, now history, would be put. These questions involved cultural identity and implied a new myth—the myth of the historic past—that, while denying its political implications, would create new political tensions both within the Amanas and between Amana and the larger society.

Tourism

THE tourist has appeared to some as a particularly modern figure, temporarily homeless, traveling, open to new experiences and sensations. Tourism has even been considered by one sociologist to be "a ritual performed to the differentiations of society . . . a way of overcoming the discontinuity of modernity."[1] While one may think that "all this is questionable, where it isn't just stuff,"[2] it is certainly true that tourism, like any structure or any ritual, does have its history—in the twentieth century one very much linked to the invention and popularization of the automobile.

HISTORY OF AMANA TOURISM

Some tourists had managed to drive their buggies through the early Ebenezer settlements, but it was the invention of the automobile that made such visitation a steady presence in the colonies. The trickle of visitors was replaced in the 1920s by a growing stream of curiosity seekers intent on seeing firsthand the quaint folk and their peculiar way of life. By the time of the Change, it is estimated that some three thousand tourists visited during the summer season, and corporation leaders early recognized the economic potential of such curiosity.[3] A 1933 *Bulletin* article encouraged readers to maintain attractive gardens instead of planting more clearly productive potato patches:

A beautiful and unique appearance of our villages will attract outsiders and tourists from coast to coast and help increase our trade and business possibilities for our mills, stores, meat markets, bakeries, and other corporation business establishments and even those of the individual.

The same issue of the *Bulletin* noted the large numbers of visitors to the community on the past Memorial Day and the business they brought to the stores. It also explained to its readers the purpose of large new signs on the community's borders: "The main idea is to welcome visitors and invite them to stop at the local filling station for further information about the Colonies, also mentioning some of the Amana products." At that time little concern was expressed about this welcoming of outsiders, a turnabout indeed from the earlier exclusionist policy.

Similar notes about the beneficent presence of tourists appear throughout the 1930s. In 1937, for example, the *Bulletin* noted that "In the near future an electric sign will be put up at the Sandwich Shop so that the tourists who pass by in the evening cannot miss the place where the best refreshments, sandwiches, luncheons, and a great variety of Amana products are sold." In 1938 a Federal Writers' Project travel book devoted eight pages to Amana; in 1940 tourists from New York reported seeing the exhibition of Amana woolens at the World's Fair.

World War II slowed tourism, but during the 1950s more and more tourists started visiting the Amanas. Widespread prosperity, improved roads and facilities and, within Amana, the opening of several restaurants offering family style meals, and the growing popularity of woolens and refrigeration products all contributed to this rise. In 1954 two community women started giving tours of the villages, and in 1955 the Amana Home museum celebrated its opening.

It was only in the 1960s, however, that the Amanas became more organized in their response to tourism and more aggressive in seeking it out.[4] Until then the state of Iowa had done little to encourage tourism: it was the last state to form a special travel division. In the early sixties, however, certain forces were spreading the concept of and the means for tourist promotion. The American Petroleum Institute was particularly active in stimulating discussion; at a special governor's conference it pushed the idea of tourist trails. One such trail, the Hiawatha Trail, wound through two thousand miles of road and four states, and one of its highlights was the Amana Colonies. The plans for the trail, which became reality, were made final and announced to the public by the governor of Iowa, Harold Hughes, in the Amana Colonies. Again, little concern was expressed.

Two Amana men, one a restaurant owner, the other later to start his own restaurant, viewed with interest these developments on the state level. Realizing that tourist development in the Amanas had taken place in a purely haphazard fashion, they were instrumental in forming the Travel Council in 1964 to help guide and promote the development of Amana tourism. Since its inception the council has sought a balance of representation among the Amana Society and various private businesses, including the restaurants, shops, wineries, and service stations. From its minutes and notes it appears to have seen its purpose as twofold: first, to promote tourism, ensuring that the Amanas, in an often used phrase, "get their fair share," and second, to involve the community ("community development") in its efforts, with the idea that the Amanas should be a pleasant place both to visit and to live.

Thus as early as 1963 the Travel Council sought to convince residents that their own interests would be served through a "successful tourist program." A *Bulletin* article that was part of a series on tourist promotion made the following points:

1. Tourists contribute to our economy and do not deprive us of facilities which are set aside for our own use, nor impose on our privacies.
2. Tourists require large quantities of various products and a great deal of services. Many people in the Amanas are employed and engaged in providing these facilities.
3. In addition to employment and attraction of tourists to the Amana Colonies, tourism provides added revenue that is brought from the outside; also the tourist is the taxpayer's friend.
4. Tourists visiting the Amana Colonies will respect our customs and heritage and do nothing to interfere with these traditions.

Optimistic, to say the least. Yet this desire to put a good face on economic interest and to solicit support continued through other

articles that told residents what they could do to ensure a successful tourist program, advice that included the following points:

1. We must sell ourselves first.
2. Show our famous brand of "Amana Hospitality."
3. Preservation.
4. We must plan together for our future.

In the early 1970s, however, some residents began expressing
their belief that the council's activities during the 1960s—devising a system of directional arrows within the Amanas, publishing
a guide map to businesses and historic attractions—had led to a
saturation of tourism, an overutilization of historic resources that
would in time deplete them.

The most organized opposition has come from a youth group
that calls itself optimistically "Unsere Hoffnungen für Unsere
Heimat" (Our Hopes for Our Homeplace). The trigger for its
founding came in the early 1970s when one son of an Amana
family made a visit to Germany, where he was touched by what
appeared to him a vision of what the old Amana might have
looked like without tourists and neon signs. He returned and
with friends founded UHUH in 1974. Drawing its membership
mostly from those aged eighteen to thirty-four, the group started
out criticizing what its young members perceived to be the
overcommercialization of the Amanas. As the president stated,
"There was the realization of the young people that the older people were exhausting the Amana name, and that we would have
nothing left." It was an interesting idea to be sure, with overtones
of the goose that laid the golden eggs. He went on to explain:

We were founded for two reasons. First, we were becoming too commer-
cialized and, second, our culture was being lost. We believed there existed a causal relationship between these two facts. Before, we had been
an isolated group of people. Now, we had roughly three-quarters of a mil-
lion people coming through annually. Our traditions, our *Gemütlichkeit*,
feeling of being one people, were being lost. The people who were profit-
ing from this were just interested in what would make money, not in
providing constructive developments. They were just mining the deeds
of our forefathers, but that heritage belongs to us all.

With this goal laid out and the energies of its youth engaged,
UHUH might have become a rallying point for opposition to tour-

ism and a revitalization of Amana culture. But the "*Kitz*," as they are referred to in Amana, appeared more interested in winning the approval of authority than in protesting against it, switching their activities from criticism of the commercial trend in general and the Travel Council in particular to activities that reflected "a more positive action" such as performing at the now-defunct Oktoberfest, itself a major part of the commercial trend. Effective opposition would prove unlikely, if simply because many members were sons and daughters or at least nieces and nephews of society directors, Church Society elders, or members operating tourist businesses. For another, the group's social functions soon took precedence over the political. As one member said, "We like to party." Oldsters—defined as those over thirty—were quietly discouraged or not notified of meeting times. And, third, the possible political impact was limited because most decisions are made by the corporation, in which UHUH members are still too young to hold stock.

The ease with which negative commentary was transformed into positive contribution suggests that no fundamental value conflict between UHUH members and the Amana business community was involved. Instead, we see reflected more of the generational tension outlined by Vidich and Bensman in *Small Town in Mass Society*. There the old local leadership was challenged by a younger generation of men, some of whom had studied or worked outside the community, many of whom were World War II veterans. In Amana, with a similar passing of command between old guard and modern leadership already accomplished, a still younger generation is waiting in the wings, giving notice that it is looking forward to assuming control. For that day it wants to be certain that the Amana legacy will be intact. The same things the older generation values—the comfortable mix of community intimacy and economic opportunity—this younger generation values. UHUH was successful in drawing attention to the danger of commercial overexploitation and in emphasizing the cultural heritage of the Amanas at a time when Amana residents, like many Americans, were eager to rediscover their roots.

RESPONSE TO TOURISM

As for the residents at large, reaction to tourism occurs on several levels: first, as a topic of conversation. A favorite after-dinner topic during informal family visits or over-the-fence chats is any variation on "Do you know what the tourists did today?" Favorite atrocities include a tourist's mistakenly entering a private home and demanding to know when dinner would be served, others trampling peony beds and picking fruit off the trees, too much photographing of "natives," and blocking private driveways with campers and vans. Those who resent the commotion the most are the elderly. A sampler:

So many people stop to take pictures of our house. I guess it's because of the flowers. Once I came out and they were having lunch under our tree! Another time I was expecting my son-in-law and I looked out on our bench by the window there and I said, I wonder why he's sitting on the bench instead of coming in, but no, it wasn't him, it was some tourist, sitting right there on our bench.

The atmosphere. There's no atmosphere any more. It used to be so peaceful.

It's only the last eight years that the tourists have gotten so bad. It's not as bad here in Homestead as it is in Main, but still; here we have Bill Zuber's Restaurant and Die Heimat Motor Hotel, and other businesses as well.

The tourists. Oh, it's awful. At least here in West we are lucky. We don't have any major road going through. Oh, once in a while we get some kids acting crazy, but mostly it's quiet. We sit outside and we can hear way down there when the pigs stick their snouts through the trough and the cover hits. I say, better that than the tourists.

On a second level, the tourist impact involves not so much the discourtesies of the few as simply the presence of the many. They take over the town and thus determine the economy. Their presence encourages further change in and possible destruction of both physical and social environment. This much may be seen on a typical Amana day. The early mornings belong to the residents. By eight o'clock most residents are up and at work: the few exercise fanatics have already biked or jogged to the nearest village and back, those not at work are busy sweeping steps and curbs or weeding their gardens. They may try to squeeze in a quick trip to the village store for milk or gossip, but by nine o'clock the first tourist cars arrive, and by ten it's already hard to find a parking place at the store. By noon full tours are making their way through museum and mill, and most residents have retreated indoors. But by five o'clock the process reverses itself. Most tourists, having seen what they came to see, eaten hearty meals, and bought a sample bottle of wine and maybe some gifts at the Christmas Shop, make their way out across the Iowa River. For the present, only one small hotel operates in Homestead. The lack of in-colony accommodations means that by six o'clock the villages once again belong to the residents, except for the occasional annoyance of a motorcycle group whizzing through, usually dismissed as "Just some kids acting crazy."

Curiously, while many residents decry the physical destruction this daily invasion causes, few are willing to take steps to limit the proliferation of tourist business. This may be because the tourist/resident encounter also involves shared American values. To some extent Amana residents are able to recognize the tourists as their own kind, like themselves when they travel. The tourists, mostly from the midwestern states, believe in families; and Amana caters to the idea of the "family vacation." They believe in education; Amana promises "an educational experience." They tell each other "It's good for us to see how they lived"; and Amana works to safeguard at least part of its heritage for future generations. Paradoxically, however, Amana as a community is unwilling to resort to the value systems of the past to protect the past, is unwilling to call up the communal and religious traditions to regulate or at least temper the current tourist abuses. The tourist, individualist par excellence, demands to see what is to be seen, to cut his or her own path even while moving in a tourist pack. Having accepted the individualistic principle in 1932, Amana residents stand helpless, except for the regulatory power granted their corporation, to work out more communal or village-centered methods to curb tourism's power to co-opt community past and present.

THE MARKETING OF AMANA

In truth one need not even visit the colonies to have a taste of their history. In the early 1970s, the Amana Society opened two "Amana stores" in Des Moines. Today one store remains. There, amid the rustic chic of exposed wooden beams and blown-up photographs of Amana craftsmen and schoolchildren, the shopper can choose among goods—some made in Amana, some elsewhere—that reflect the new trend toward an international marketing of folklore. Amana rockers and cabinets stand next to imported leather backgammon sets, Royal Doulton porcelain figurines, papier-mâché boxes from India, and straw chicken music boxes from the People's Republic of China. Amana meat products in the refrigerated case are set off by French cookie cutters, Italian ice cream spades, and Ghirardelli chocolates. The most popular goods include the Amana foodstuffs and the community's woolen and wooden products. For it is truly the Amana myth that attracts the shoppers. Some, excited by the aura of craftsmanship in the shop, decide to make the two-hour trip from Des Moines to see the real community. Other potential tourists are drawn off Route 80 by signs for the "Little Amana" Holiday Inn tourist complex, where they can spend the night, breakfast in one of the restaurant's famous "buggy booths," and tour the shops by the motel. Part of the rationale for this complex was the hope of protecting the actual villages from commercial overexploitation and traffic congestion. Some tourists staying one night or enjoying a meal at Little Amana believe they have seen one of the colonies, though most realize that this former communal society lies some five miles north of the interstate.

There are two ways of approaching the Amanas from the interstate: on a well-maintained, smoothly paved state road that travels past small neighboring Conroy and down into South Amana, or on a potholed roller coaster of a gravel county road. For those intrepid tourists who ignore the instructions in the Little Amana Holiday Inn brochures, the gravel road offers an appropriate entrance and a possible vision of Amana past. After hours on the highway, the change to clouds of dust and the clatter of gravel bouncing off sheet metal is accentuated, and one thinks back to horse-and-buggy days when these miles of gravel and dirt protected Amana from outsiders. The first sight of Homestead is peaceful enough, off to the right past fields and pastureland, but where gravel road meets paved thoroughfare a huge sign for Bill Zuber's Dugout Restaurant reminds one how much this village, and the other six, have changed over time.

A tour of the villages might well start there in Homestead, where tourists can choose between the Zuber restaurant and another. They may start their round of museums with the Amana Heim museum, which, strangely enough, includes a private kitchen and seems to be laid out for a nuclear family instead of one extended family or several small families.

Next door is the Blacksmith Shop, where tourists can buy ice cream, and next to that is the (fairly) authentic Homestead Meat Market, where traditional sausages and meats compete with the not-so-traditional postcards and candies. Other Homestead businesses geared completely or in part to tourists include Alma's Wash House—a gift and antique shop—and the first of the many wineries in the villages.

The main tourist action, however, is in the next village the tourists are likely to hit—Amana, known as "Main" or "Big" Amana to residents. Here cars and trailers line both sides of the street, parked up against the Bread and Pastry Shop offering "*Pretzeln, Brot, und Kuchen*"; Der Wein Keller, the Antique Tower House, and several other gift shops. The General Store stocks many tourist items along with goods for the community. Main Amana also boasts the major meat market, but the greatest attractions are the three family-style restaurants. Another central feature is the woolen mill, where guided tours leave every hour and where a salesroom offers a fine selection of fabrics made on the premises. Next to the woolen mill is the Original Amana Furniture and Clock Shop. Again tours are given, and the major pieces of furniture are so popular that a special order may take some time to fill. With all these businesses competing for the tourists' attention, many also find an hour or so to tour the Museum of Amana History.

East Amana offers no special attraction other than its hazy bucolic atmosphere, so most tourists pass it by, making their way instead to Middle Amana, where the community kitchen and cooper-shop museum await them, along with the old hearth bakery, still in use. Another winery and another gift shop, a glance at the refrigeration plant down the hill, then it's on to High and West Amana a couple of miles down the road. These again are smaller villages: tourists visit the High Amana store and the furniture repair shop, gift shop, and broom and basket shops at the foot of the hill in West. On across the river to South Amana. Here, besides another restaurant and gift shop, a Barn Museum was opened to display farm equipment, buggies, and tools used by the colonists as well as to serve as workshop and display area for a collection of crafted models of "Amana and Americana in Miniature," suggestive of the interpenetration of communal and national myths.

For souvenirs there are of course postcards, featuring among other sites the lily lake, the meat market—"Amana Colonies: Bratwurst Capital of the World"—and the South Amana flower gardens—"These Sugar Daddy petunias and apple trees help make South Amana, Iowa, a lovely place to visit." For the children there used to be an Amana coloring book with an "Amana-Go-Round" game on the back cover; players made their way around the seven villages by flipping a coin; tails and you sat out your turn in the lily lake. Among all the other ways of merchandizing the Amana past, this coloring book might seem the height of trivialization: the lily lake, a community landmark, turned into a board game. In many of these sites and some of these products there is a serious effort to educate and communicate, but also involved is the translation of history into commodity, a process that seriously alters the community's actual political content.

Underneath the product we can detect a myth and a message, but it is not always the inspiration of Metz that is being communicated. A folding packet of twelve color photographs calls the Amanas "a unique combination of modern efficiency and old world traditions. Its products and people reflecting the best of the old and the best of the new." Many community people would like to believe and to have it believed that they do enjoy "the best of both worlds," that they have kept the warmth and security of the old way of life but added to it efficiency and mobility, increased leisure and broader horizons. They take off for lengthy vacations and Florida condominiums, only to return proclaiming the beauty of their Amana landscape.

Further underneath the marketing and the message the moral lies half hidden. What is the particular attraction of former utopias? What is it that Amana shares with the Shaker communities, and with Oneida, and with the Amish, whose Lancaster settlements form the seventh largest tourist attraction in the United States? It may well be that these communities function as morality plays to the industrial age. They serve as human dramas in which the players struggle to keep the devil—whatever form it may assume—beyond their gates and out of their hearts. They serve purposes both cathartic and ideological. When such communities succeed, we applaud what we read as their high-minded goodness and biblical faith. In a sense they take the burden of idealism off our shoulders. When they fail we regret it much as we regret the ending of a tragedy, yet call it inevitable. For there is no stopping progress and no alternative. Our historic choices thus assume the aura of irrevocable fate. E. M. Forster realized on a visit to a Shaker settlement that his American friends were much more touched than he by the experience. He attributed their interest in the Shakers to the mythical power of the American dream, a dream "that got bogged, the dream of an America which should be in direct touch with the elemental and the simple. America has chosen the power that comes through machinery, but she never forgets her dream."[5] As in a morality play, the Inspirationists, like the Shakers, present the major themes of our cultural myth, and though we sense the possibility the ending itself is never in doubt. Their limited successes fill us with nostalgia for the "elemental and the simple." Their failures teach us that we need not try ourselves.

In the 1930s society drew from Amana the moral that communism's best chance had failed. In the 1980s the message is more complex, revolving around the inevitability of the modern despite the felt loss of the past. We visit this past, preserving its artifacts while denying its critical content. This myth has nonetheless given rise to political structures and tensions: between residents themselves, between tourists and residents, between residents and representatives of the national culture—museum curators, architects, government officials. The myth is of the past; the politics are very much of the present. This much can be seen in a second issue now facing the Amanas, the issue of historic preservation.

Historic Preservation

I F one were playing devil's advocate, one might suggest that the easiest, if most drastic, solution would be for the Amana residents to sacrifice one village to the tourists, leaving a *cordon sanitaire* between the museum and the modern. As it is, a shaky balance exists between these two forces within the seven villages.

Amana people have been of two minds about the historicity of their community. For a long time many felt embarrassed by the "quaintness" of their villages; but with the rise of prosperity and much social integration they are now taking pride in their cultural heritage. This response itself is not without its ambiguities and complexities. The debate over historic preservation has stirred up deep fears of going backward—conceived specifically as back to dusty streets and elder control, but more generally as the antithesis of progress and the negation of earlier choices. The debate has also stirred up questions regarding the historic: What is it? Whence comes its element of sanctity? Does the past demand preservation, or is it a millstone weighing down those who want to make their own choices?

The preservationist argument is based partly on the idea that, if we destroy the physical community and its artifacts, all we can trust to for our appreciation of the past are other people's interpretations. The argument carries particular force in the Amanas, where the physical environment was once so distinctive. The village layout is reminiscent of the European rather than the American countryside, with houses and barns clustered on land ill suited for agriculture. The architecture also is distinctive, the plain wooden, brick, and sandstone structures originally having only flowers, trellises, and fruit trees for ornament. But few of the old structures have been left in their pure state. An architect researching the Amanas was dismayed by the turn individualism had taken in the residents' attempts to personalize their homes:

Now it seems that Amana residents themselves have come to undervalue their collective heritage. The Great Change of 1932 gave individuals their own houses and shares of stock in Amana corporations; current prosperity results from corporate success with tourism as much as with wool and refrigerators. Individual remodelings and renovations reflect both prosperity and the long stifled desire for personal expression. Brick houses flash decorative aluminum screen doors, stone houses receive additions sheathed in blue aluminum siding. . . . Restaurants in the old kitchen houses acquire plastic paneled interiors and neon signs; ornamental ducks and wheelbarrows sit on the lawns. Each building so transformed is subtracted from the village, set apart from the tight network of original houses, churches, mills, and barns. Because Amana's architecture lacks symbolic display, it is especially vulnerable to this crass remodeling: demolition would be almost kinder.[1]

In addition to the architectural desecration of the old buildings, the visual integrity of the landscape is slowly being destroyed by new buildings of varied design. Much of this construction dates from the immediate postwar period, when returning GI's and other young people acted on their preference for modern-style houses. "Boystown," a development of ranch and split level houses in Main Amana, was built during this period and was soon followed by a "Girlstown" development of similar housing across the highway. Other areas in Homestead, Middle Amana, and High Amana have been taken over by these new structures, often attractive but visually jarring.

There is also, finally, the effect on the visual environment of the tourist enterprises and their taste in signs. Little regulation exists: establishments post signs running the gamut from neon monstrosities to small hand-painted wooden placards. The varied appearance of the businesses and residences reflects to some extent the people's ambivalence toward their distinctive history: it is only recently that the distance from the communal past has become great enough that residents are again growing interested in it.

HISTORICAL BACKGROUND

Paradoxically, interest in community history has grown as community symbols have been destroyed and new ones substituted. Shortly after the Change, electrification came to the Amanas, both remodeling Amana interiors and altering the landscape with electric poles. Residents rushed to change their houses' exteriors as well, paying little attention to the *Bulletin*'s suggestion that "all such changes be in harmony with our colonial style. Any radical deviation from this would naturally react on the eye in the same manner as a false note in music reacts on the ear." Other symbols of the Amana landscape were being lost. During World War I the Amanas lost a valued pine forest when the United States government asked for wood for guns. Although Amana men maintained their traditional pacifist stance during that war, their pacifism did not prevent this contribution to the national war effort. In the late 1930s a beloved stand of twenty-eight maple trees in Homestead was cut down, and the West Amana flour mill was discontinued, as were many of the small village craft shops. New and larger businesses opened.

In the postwar era interest in community history started its slow revival. A cookbook of traditional Amana recipes appeared, and a popular nostalgia column won a place in the *Bulletin*. The Amana Heim Museum opened in 1955, the same year the community celebrated the centennial of its arrival in Iowa. But, in the loss column, other symbols were on the way out in the 1950s: the horse-drawn funeral, the Upper South store. New structures—the split levels and ranches—appeared, destroying the coherent village landscape. The necessity for instituting English church services, already discussed, reflects the declining use of the most complicated symbol system, the Amana dialect. Even food patterns went through changes symbolic of a changing community. Just as the break from eating in communal kitchens symbolized the decline of communalism, so too a comparison of Amana cookbooks suggests a move from the highly traditional German fare to a cuisine drawing its inspiration equally from history and the pages of *Good Housekeeping*. A recently published cookbook entitled *Favorite Amana Recipes* includes, along with *Schmierkäse*, liver dumplings, and red cabbage, recipes for jello cookies, pineapple whipped cream salad, and ice cream soup.

Despite this continued penetration by national culture, or perhaps in response to it, a revival of community has been occurring in the guise of historic preservation, a program and process that turns the old into myth—chicken coops become symbolic—while offering economic and political incentives for its protection. Interestingly, the impetus for much of the preservationist activity in Amana came first from the outside. Largely through the efforts of the Iowa State Historical Society, the Department of the Interior Park Service conferred National Historic Landmark status on the community in a ceremony held in 1966. At the time of this award the community had no appropriate place to display the plaque, so for several years it stayed mounted on a pedestal outside the Amana Welfare Clubhouse.

Although it was outside agencies that conferred official historic status upon Amana, individuals and organizations within the community had begun thinking along the lines of preserving some aspects of the old. At the urging of the Travel Council president, in 1966 the Amana Society purchased an old house situated at the entrance to Main Amana, with a view to converting it into a museum. While the expectation was that the Travel Council would accomplish the conversion, for almost two years little happened. Thus in 1968 the Society pushed for an organization formed expressly to create the museum. Four community women spearheaded this effort, and to them belongs much of the credit. Whereas at first converting the house into a museum seemed impossible, residents pitched in, volunteering time and artifacts, and outside experts willingly gave their professional advice. Today the museum is a major attraction and has extended to include three buildings, extensive displays, and a film presentation.

The organization responsible both for starting the museum and for its continued operation is the Amana Heritage Society.[2] With representatives drawn from the major Amana organizations

(Amana Society, Amana Church Society, the Travel Council, UHUH), it sees its purpose as both preserving the Amana past and interpreting it for visitors. With the establishment of the museum, the preservation of artifacts was assured. As the years passed, however, the Heritage Society came to realize that it had a far greater task than mere artifact preservation.

No one could be blind to changes in the Amana landscape. The Heritage Society soon became concerned with historic buildings that were suffering from years of neglect. After a few tentative steps to rescue first this building, then that one, the group realized that preservation on the scale demanded was too great a project to fit under the functions it has originally outlined for itself. After considerable discussion, a second committee was formed with some overlapping of membership, calling itself the Amana Historic Landmark Committee.

The minutes of the Landmark Committee reflect a learning process similar to that experienced by the Heritage Society. Outside experts, including specialists from the nearby Herbert Hoover Presidential Library and National Historic Site, were called in to assist in renovating the buildings and setting up displays. In similar fashion the Landmark Committee received advice on how the new Amana should come to terms with the old, on how it should negotiate its encounter with the past.

THE DEVELOPMENT OF A MASTER PLAN

In the two years following the Landmark Committee's founding in 1974, experts from the Hoover museum and the State Historical Society came to talk on such subjects as preservation legislation and funding, problems of "maintaining the historic identity of a community in the face of social change and economic expansion," and the importance of recruiting even more specialists to develop a long-range preservation plan. Slowly the committee was weaned from its piecemeal approach of restoring first one building, then another and convinced that a "master plan" was in order. One architectural historian associated with the State Historical Department went so far as to claim that Amana had "more potential now than Williamsburg did before its restoration" and that "if there is a place worth saving it would be Amana." Convinced, the committee requested funds from the corporation and Church Society to match the $12,500 allotted by the State Historical Department to hire preservation planners. Funds received, it set about screening planners whose names were on the State Historical Department list of firms experienced in community restoration.

The lengthy process of interviewing firms and reviewing applications ended in March 1977 with the selection of a young group from Charlottesville, Virginia, called Land and Community Associates. The small firm had already worked on planning problems facing a historic nineteenth-century city (Cumberland, Maryland), two rural Appalachian counties (Highland and Bath counties, Virginia), and a critical island area (the town of Tangier, Virginia).[3]

Before the team arrived in spring 1977, the committee members conducted a small informal survey of resident opinion. While the survey would hardly stand up under scientific scrutiny, it is nonetheless suggestive of the contradictory attitudes residents held toward restoration of their villages. Most of the 395 respondents preferred to have the Amanas look as they do today rather than at any earlier time, and many commented that one could hardly tear down the buildings that had been erected in recent years. Yet they also hoped that some restraints could be placed on future building. The sentiment was strong for some form of guidelines, as the responses to the following questions indicate:

1. Are you in favor of some kind of long range plan for historic preservation and restoration of the Amana Colonies? 84% yes
2. Would you be in favor of certain guidelines in the location of new buildings? 75% yes
3. Are you in favor of the restoration and preservation of selected barns and other buildings of historic interest and [of putting them] to a functional purpose? 86% yes

These responses suggest a community mandate to the planners to proceed with their work, and yet, as one individual reflected afterward, "It's a lot easier to say you're for something on a questionnaire than to back it and contribute to make it reality." There were hidden layers of opposition to a return, however negotiated.

During the fieldwork stage, the project directors made every effort to coax out sentiments and determine possible opposition, meeting with every segment of the population separately and in special village meetings held in each village church. At these village meetings, the directors encouraged participation by asking residents to verify their understanding of the pre-1932 appearance of the villages. At the Main Amana meeting residents complained of the uncontrolled parking and unsightly billboards; in East Amana residents demanded the village remain quietly residential. In High Amana people wanted to preserve their agricultural complex, even if it meant turning the old barns into a residential area, and in Homestead the major concern was the "poor visual quality" of business establishments and the major desire to prevent any new visitor-oriented businesses. The other villages indicated similar concern over regulating or prohibiting commercial establishments, maintaining historic buildings, and the need to regulate signs and parking throughout the colonies.

The firm also conducted a brief survey of tourist opinion. Most of the visitors listed their home states as Wisconsin, Indiana, Michigan, Ohio, Iowa, Missouri, Nebraska, and Kansas. The attractions they enjoyed most during their stay included the restaurants, furniture factory, Heritage Museum, barn museum, woolen mill, and wineries, and simply viewing the historic buildings. And some tourists, a "substantial minority," expressed disappointment with their visit, sources of which included, "the overcommercial character and appearance. . . , the lack of parking, the large numbers of non-Amana items offered for sale, the lack of public facilities such as restrooms and drinking fountains, the modernization of historic buildings, and the scarcity of existing interpretive activities and materials." The tourists were, in short, demanding both facilities and authenticity, two things that they apparently did not see as contradictory. They wanted a community untouched by their presence and yet catering to it.

Nonetheless, this was what the planners wanted to hear and what they would try to provide. After several months of fieldwork the team returned to its Virginia base to prepare the master plan, which was completed and presented to the community in spring 1978. The plan was then discussed at village meetings similar to the ones held during the fieldwork stage, and copies of the plan, entitled "Culture and Environment: A Challenge for the Amana Colonies," were placed in the museum library, available for borrowing.

THE PLAN ITSELF

The plan was outstanding in its scope and thoroughness. Its general framework emphasized centralization of functions and design, as presented in the introduction:

The Amana villages have always been a system of tightly defined, densely concentrated settlements in a state where dispersed individual homesites were the rule. Today dispersal in such areas as housing, visitor circulation, and commercial development threatens the historic Amana community. The components of this plan outline the ways in which concentrations of uniformly designed structures and landscapes, clearly defined and concentrated commercial areas, and concentrations of visitor-related services and facilities, can improve both visual quality and quality of life in the Amanas through the cooperative efforts of the Amana people, the Amana Society, and other groups which make decisions about Amana's environment.

This framework was seen as comprising the four components of visual quality and order, growth and development, interpretation and circulation, and community spirit and awareness. Under visual quality the report stressed both historical reminders—"the plowed fields, the forests, the layout of the seven Amana villages"—and the changes affecting this vision, such as the new housing developments or the problem of uncontrolled signs. Under growth and development the report emphasized both commercial and residential growth. By interpretation and circulation the plan meant finding better ways to present Amana history to tourists and to regulate the flow of pedestrians and vehicles. Finally, the report also stressed the importance of heightened community awareness if the program of regulation and development were to succeed. These general points received little attention. It was the specifics that became the focus of community discussion and dissent.

The specific suggestions ranged from colonywide recommendations down to recommendations for each separate village and
also included several "specific projects." For example, at the
colonywide level there were suggestions to establish historic districts, develop a uniform sign system, replant some fields with
historically authentic crops, restock others with livestock types
used before 1932, create bicycle routes, and place utility lines
underground. At the village level, for the village of Main Amana
the report recommended moving the blacksmith shop back to its
original location, removing the "western front" from the General
Store, removing white paint from the Amana service station or
covering it with brick-red paint, restoring ditches and gullies
along the streets and putting back the sidewalk fences, and
changing the name of "the Wickery" to something more appro-
priately German, such as "Korbmacher-Shop" or simply "Baskets." Such specific suggestions for each village were more controversial than the somewhat bland general principles. Receiving
the most attention, however, were two of the "special projects":
first, building an "eighth village," and second, looking into the
possibility of becoming historic districts.

The planners saw the creation of an eighth village on Amana
land as one way to control the new building without forbidding it
altogether. Their report called for a contest to select a firm to design the layout and housing of this new village, which was to be
contemporary in design yet harmonious with the historic Amana
architecture. The press picked up on this idea more than on any
other feature of the plan, clearly to the disadvantage of the plan's
proponents.

First of all, the term "eighth village" proved unfortunate. The
idea of seven villages was sacrosanct to many, especially the older
residents, and they seized upon this particular suggestion with a
vengeance reflecting their fears of what these young people—
outsiders at that—planned to do with their sacred past. "There
have always been seven villages; that's the way it's always been."
The word spread that "they" wanted to build an eighth Amana,
"they" including both planners and the preservation enthusiasts
within the Amanas. Some opponents also disliked the idea that
the design would reflect traditional village layout, including the
paths that connected individual houses and backyards. Residents

now preferred the privacy such paths denied and also insisted on their right to build exactly where they pleased. Despite the costs to the physical environment, they objected to any plan that threatened their chosen individualism. "A man's home is his castle" was all the truth the plan's critics needed.[4] Another source of criticism was the feeling that any form of control would resemble elder control, threatening individualism and the need to push forward, leaving the past behind:

You can't have the houses the way they were before—we didn't have kitchens in the houses. . . . You can't go back. I like it better now.

They want to make it like it was before, with the kitchens and the fences and all. . . . That schoolhouse over there, that couldn't be apartments like it is now. You can't go back, that's topsy-turvy, all upside down.

People own lots in Amana, now they're telling them they can't build on them, or change their houses. But people will anyway. I'm not worried. They told some of those up on Main Street they couldn't open gift shops and the people did it anyway. You can't stop them.

The fact was that no one intended to take the kitchens out of private homes, to in any way touch the interiors, or to return buildings such as the schoolhouse to their original functions. The second major "special project," the historic district idea, would, however, mean some regulation of exteriors of old structures and control over the building of new ones.

Under the Landmark status the colonies had already been granted some control over federally funded, licensed, or financially assisted projects, but no such control existed over individual buildings or alterations. Only designation as a historic district could grant the community such control over individuals' decisions. If the Amanas were to decide to become historic districts, with each village a separate district, representatives would be elected to a village historic district commission whose main power would involve regulating external changes in buildings under its control. Any individual wishing to effect a change through construction, alteration, restoration, movement, or demolition would have to receive a certificate of appropriateness from the commission. Without such a certificate the individual or business could not make the proposed changes. The commission, however, lacked enforcement powers, so if compliance were not forthcoming the disagreement would have to be brought to court. Even so, the idea that some residents might be in a position to tell other residents what they could and could not do proved threatening enough.

Today, several years after the plan's appearance, historic districts are still under discussion. But in other ways preservationist activity has generated remarkable enthusiasm. A *Volksmarsch*, an annual community walk, was instituted a few years ago and is growing in popularity. A flourishing arts and crafts program exists, highlighted by an annual fair featuring only Amana artists and craftspeople. An expert from the Iowa Arts program came to the community to teach residents how to record oral history from the older people who remember the pre-Change period. Most significantly, the old Landmark Committee developed into a nonprofit preservation organization and hired an outside expert to help supervise preservation throughout the community.

Thus the most purely cultural and individually motivated ideas have taken fastest root, with those that contain more political content, such as the historic district idea, finding the Amana soil less welcoming. This should not be a surprise, for ethnicity and culture are often enjoyed for their folkloric aspects yet feared for their political implications.[5] In Amana these political implications revolve around the fact that through tourism and the growing interest in preservation Amana is fast developing into a cultural periphery, a status that causes distinct problems for community residents. Both tourism and the historic district debate raise questions about just how far the Amanas are willing to go in institutionalizing this process and in "professionalizing" their community. The current reaction by some residents against tourism and the desire to safeguard Amana for future generations are reflected in other cultural peripheries such as Quebec, where young nationalists work to deemphasize tourist development while reemphasizing distinctiveness through political organization.[6] Amana's historic movement, from a community that lived its communalism and pietism to one that enshrines its past, thus casts a curious light on our own search for cultural identity in the modern era.

Conclusion

W̶e can now better understand how myth and politics have operated throughout Amana history and how they connect Amana's development with the development of American society. Starting first in early-eighteenth-century Germany, we have seen how political tensions between aristocrats and ministers and among the levels of the churchmen themselves gave rise to a popular religious protest that advocated a return to fundamental Christian values. The mixture of these pietist ideas with mysticism provided the legitimating ideology for the first Inspirationist cells. These cells soon found themselves at odds with the established powers because of their nonconformist theology and in particular because of their refusal to bear arms or to send their children to state schools. With the inroads made on pietism by Enlightenment thought in the later eighteenth century and the decline in religious fervor on the death of the Inspirationist leaders, the small groups were reduced in size and spirit, struggling on through the latter half of the eighteenth century.

In 1817 political conditions encouraged revival of the Inspirationist faith. Crop failures, increasing population pressure, early symptoms of industrialization, and a substantial breakdown in village life and morality encouraged some men and women to turn to pietist values. For pietism, though no longer the dominant force among intellectuals, had nonetheless remained popular among the common people. The Inspirationist ideology, encouraging a return to the values of early Christianity and to the social structures of an earlier Germany, appealed to those industrialization was leaving behind—to the old members and new converts Metz gathered on the various estates in Hesse-Darmstadt. The sect could not, however, truly segregate itself from the political tensions of its time and from the competing social forces in a Germany moving toward nationhood. State and church joined together to discourage protest, whether political, as in the case of the growing socialist opposition, or religious, as in the case of dissenting sects like the Inspirationists. The refusal of the state to grant non-German Inspirationists citizenship, combined with crop failures in 1841, encouraged Metz and the elders to consider emigration. Once again the political decision was legitimated by religion, with Metz providing the inspired testimony that sent a scouting party to America, where they approved the purchase of land in New York State.

In this period the German institutions of authority, the Lutheran church, and the provincial authorities felt threatened by the Inspirationist religion, which represented latent political opposition. In America, this religion would be the group's guarantee of toleration, making their communalism somewhat more acceptable to outside critics.

While the interweaving of religious myth and social structure fostered the growth and stability of the community during its early years in Ebenezer, the "commitment mechanisms" developed within the community were no match for the threats from outside. Buffalo residents found the Inspirationists almost as exotic as the Indians who had preceded them on the land. In this new American setting, outsiders saw the religion as quaint or old-fashioned, certainly not directly threatening to a young state that had already witnessed major religious revivals and the creation of dissenting sects. Outsiders did feel a sense of unease over the element of compulsion and the perceived loss of individualism implied by group membership, attitudes toward Amana and other communal attempts that to some extent have endured. When Inspirationists looked toward the outsiders, they also saw them as exotic and, despite strict religious proscriptions, as tempting and appealing. Adding to such social tensions were eco-

nomic ones: indeed, it seemed that the problems the Inspirationists had faced in Germany—land hunger, urbanization, competition from farms and mills of increasing scale and rational
organization—had again caught up with them. Once again the
leadership called upon the faith to legitimate a political decision:
to look westward.

As the Inspirationists settled onto their new land in Iowa, they
entered more fully into the utopia/society dialectic whereby each
social system uses the other to generate stories or myths that
help safeguard and defend its own ideology. We have seen how in
Amana the leadership repeatedly filtered outside news, accepting
and promulgating only those items that could be interpreted
as signs of God's displeasure with worldly women and men. How
the less-controlled wider society viewed the "utopia" is more
problematic.

Writing in the 1870s, that leading student of communalism
Charles Nordhoff saw groups like Amana or the Shaker settlements as offering a societal escape hatch. With the West increasingly settled and no longer the great adventure it once was, these
communes, he argued, could serve as a new frontier. Dissatisfied
elements of the lower urban classes could be encouraged to join
such societies and then resocialized according to the often stricter
morality.

Throughout the nation, interest in social experiment was
widespread during the late 1800s, and Amana's peculiar mix of
religion and socialism was seen as one workable solution among
many being offered both in social fact and in utopian fiction. Two
of the earliest students of Amana, Perkins and Wick, provide a
not untypical evaluation of the community. Commenting on how
many other communal attempts had already died out or were suffering major reversals, the authors agreed with Oneida's John
Humphrey Noyes that "mere social ties do not seem sufficiently
strong to bind men closely and firmly together."[1] The success of
the Inspirationists, especially when contrasted to the struggle of
the Icarians who came to the state of Iowa in approximately the
same period, was laid primarily to their religion:

The members have never held "that the ownership of property is a
crime," neither have they belonged to that dreamy class of idealists who

continually appeal to sentiment in order to achieve success. Their Teutonic instinct of individuality made them preserve much of their independence . . . they never belonged to that class which has nothing at stake, and therefore stirs up insurrection because they have nothing to lose and may have much to win. The Communalism of this Society has been founded upon that sober, old Christian idea of love which Christ and the Apostles gave to the world.[2]

Thus in 1891, the date of the Perkins and Wick publication, we see Amana already used as myth, the myth of a primitive Christianity combined with American individualism in opposition to the spread of godless socialist ideas. Socialism had enjoyed considerable popularity and socialists had suffered considerable persecution in the preceding decade. In this text, demonstrating what would emerge as a typical refusal to engage with conflicting political ideologies, the authors stressed how simple pragmatism, aided by religious faith, was what made Amana communism effective. Contrasting Amana religion to the utopian fabrications of Cabet, Owen, and the transcendentalist enthusiasts at Brook Farm, the authors continued:

The Amana Society, on the contrary, has never embodied these Utopian ideas; it is founded . . . upon a basis more sober and less fanciful; it does not endeavor to make human beings more perfect than humanity is capable of being. . . . If Communism can ever be successful it must proceed upon its way in accordance with the limitations of human nature; it can not reckon upon the attributes of character which might belong to angels, but are not found among men. . . . The failure of most Communistic societies may be traced to the unpractical, theoretical, and inchoate ideas of their founders, to the false views of human nature which have usurped the place of true ones, and to the belief that the prejudices of humanity may be, in an instant, reformed or annulled by circumstances. The falsity of this doctrine has been proved over and over again, and human nature remains today very much the same as in the time of Plato.[3]

In the fabrication of myth from the raw material of history, the term "human nature" has often provided a convenient short-circuiting of more complicated logic and argument. It aids the process whereby, as Barthes suggests, the contradictions and complexities of history are removed and the outcomes assume an inevitable cast. Continuing in this strain, outsiders in the 1920s would view it as "natural" that the colonists would rebel against Inspirationism, though earlier viewers would have seen it as equally "natural" that they were sustained by their faith and communal structure. Outsiders considered it "natural" that young people would leave family and friends to seek opportunities outside the community, for they increasingly saw the youth of their own small towns looking toward broader horizons. Similarly swayed by their own concerns and totally misjudging the Inspirationist tradition of pacifism, some outsiders viewed it as "natural" that these German colonists refused to fight German soldiers in World War I, and they harassed the communards by way of punishment.

In 1932, however, such political grievances were forgotten. Amana had chosen the right path, the natural path. Its whole history could now serve as myth, especially since it served first to juxtapose and then to resolve the tensions between two dominant American myths: the static myth of the garden embodied in the rural past and the dynamic myth of progress symbolized by the self-made man. Once again it was human nature that served to bridge the gap between these two competing myths. The Great Change was thereby reduced to a pragmatic business decision: "Then they took a practical view of the thing and decided that the capitalistic system . . . was the system under which they best could pursue their business of farming and milling."[4] From the late 1930s right through the 1950s, Amana's continued success symbolized to many Americans capitalism's continued economic success. After World War II Amana history rendered into myth was especially popular as cold war propaganda, particularly noticeable on the occasion of Khrushchev's visit to Des Moines, Iowa.

Today Amana continues to serve as a myth. No longer totally enchanted with the image and goods of modernity, many Americans look back at the Amana myth not for vindication of the modern way of life but for a nostalgic glimpse of the American past. Some are even more consciously looking backward to the old Amana in order to look forward to a different America. This reinterpretation gained force in the 1960s as the theme of the loss of community became popular in social science literature and as young people studied examples of past communal attempts and created their own alternative societies. But it was not just the young who succumbed to visions of communities past: to others Amana appeared as the mythical small town taken to the extreme, as a sort of heightened community where people were somehow better because they were forced by norms and circumstance to be better.

Now idyllic visions of a communal past still delight, despite the contrasting recent evidence of Jonestown and other totalitarian religious cults. Today the perceived goodness and simplicity of the near-extinct Shaker villages, the transformed Amana Colonies, and the still-thriving Hutterite settlements serve as mythic support for the "small is beautiful" philosophy. Discussing the recent move of Mennonites and Amish people to New York State in search of inexpensive land, one scholar remarked:

Only a few years ago the Amish were perceived as an impediment to progress. They were pictured as a backward people who didn't understand the importance of continued economic growth, more advanced technology, and a progressive education. Today, when the need for limiting growth is as uncritically accepted in some quarters as was the previous mandate for sustained growth, the Amish philosophy of smallness and plainness is frequently extolled and less frequently emulated.[5]

The value of Amana as myth thus can be traced to its interweaving of the two myths, first, of the agrarian paradise; second, of technological progress. Depending on the political and social tensions and the ideological demands of the moment, the national mythmakers, including media spokesmen and political leaders, and the American people, as tourists and seekers, turn to whichever aspect of Amana history best provides new answers or reinforces old ones.

Indeed, given this tendency to translate history into myth, we may be led to ask whether we can ever truly approach history on its own terms, without recourse to dominant cultural myths. Roland Barthes would suggest not, that instead we continually drift between our attraction to the historical object of study and our need to demystify it. "For if we penetrate the object, we liberate it but we destroy it; and if we acknowledge its full weight, we respect it, but we restore it to a state which is still mystified."[6] Nonetheless, he would still argue that such an attempt must be made, such a "reconciliation between reality and myth, between description and explanation, between object and knowledge." If we could succeed in so approaching the past, succeed, as Paul Ricoeur suggests, in understanding "that the entirety of human existence is a text to be read," and if we approach it as both believer and atheist, we may yet return to communities like Amana their critical content, thus restoring their original voice while adding our own interpretive contributions. As Ricoeur describes the effort: "If we can no longer live the great symbolisms . . . in accordance with the original belief in them, we can, we modern men, aim at a second naïveté in and through criticism. In short, it is by interpreting that we can hear again."[7] In this process, in our trying both "to exist in the world as an individual being, to pursue a historical adventure in a humanity that seeks to become whole," Amana will always interest, in part for its own historical drama, in part for what it reflects of our national course and our individual choices.

Notes

PREFACE

1. Charles Péguy, *Basic Verities* (New York: Pantheon, 1943), p. 108.
2. Roland Barthes, *Mythologies* (New York: Hill and Wang, 1972), p. 143.
3. Victor W. Turner and Edith Turner, *Image and Pilgrimage in Christian Culture: Anthropological Perspectives* (New York: Columbia University Press, 1978), p. 20.

CHAPTER I

1. Historians of religion remind us that there exist different brands of pietism, including Moravian, Swabian, and Calvinist pietism as well as pietism as a reform movement within the Lutheran church. See Horst Weigelt, "Interpretations of Pietism in the Research of Contemporary German Church Historians," *Church History* 39 (1970): 236–41
2. For sources on the early German history of the Inspirationists, see my Bibliographical Essay.
3. F. L. Carsten, *Princes and Parliaments in Germany* (Oxford: Oxford University Press, 1959).
4. Eda Sagarra, *A Social History of Germany, 1648–1840* (London: Methuen, 1977), p. 110.
5. Ibid. p. 111.
6. Although Burke fails to provide figures for Germany, he does tell us that in Amsterdam in 1630 the male literacy rate was 57 percent, a figure that by 1780 had risen to 85 percent. In Normandy the literacy rate

rose from 10 percent to 80 percent in the course of the eighteenth century, and it was even higher in Sweden. Burke writes, "In short, printed matter was accessible to a good many craftsmen and peasants in this period, even if we cannot say whether 'a good many' was more or less than 50 percent, let alone calculate—given their fragility—how many broadsides and chapbooks there were." See Peter Burke, *Popular Culture in Early Modern Europe* (London: Temple Smith, 1978), pp. 251–52.

7. Hajo Holborn, *A History of Modern Germany, 1648–1840* (London: Eyre and Spottiswoode, 1965), p. 138.

8. Ibid., p. 136.

9. Gottfried Scheuner, the Inspirationist scholar, and anthropologist Jonathan Andelson differ somewhat on the timing of meetings during these early years. See Janet Zuber's translation of Gottfried Scheuner's *Inspirations-Histories*, published by the Amana Society (1977), and Jonathan Gary Andelson, "Communalism and Change in the Amana Colonies" (Ph.D. dissertation, University of Michigan, 1974).

10. Sagarra, *Social History of Germany*. There is some debate about the principle and practice of equality within pietism. While Sagarra emphasizes the social egalitarianism of pietists, John Gagliardo believes that the pietists, although often perceived as social levelers, nonetheless often supported the predominant corporate view of society as composed of interlocking classes or estates. See John G. Gagliardo, *From Pariah to Patriot: The Changing Image of the German Peasant, 1770–1840* (Lexington: University of Kentucky Press, 1969).

11. The community record for the first two years reflects considerable instability, with various members claiming inspiration. What emerges by 1718, however, is a clear leadership struggle among four *Werkzeuge*, with Rock and Ursula Mayer teamed up against the younger Johann Gleim and Gruber's son. Rock and Mayer prevail (though Mayer loses her inspiration in 1719), and Gleim and Gruber Jr. leave the community, Gruber emigrating to Pennsylvania. It is also interesting that in 1726 one of the leading community members suggested emigration to the United States, but this was vetoed by Rock, then secure in his leadership.

12. Bertha Shambaugh, *Amana That Was and Amana That Is* (Iowa City: State Historical Society of Iowa).

13. Sidney E. Ahlstrom, *A Religious History of the American People* (New Haven: Yale University Press, 1972), p. 241.

14. Holborn, *History of Modern Germany*, p. 141.

15. See Gottlieb Scheuner, *Inspirations-Historie*, vol. 1, trans. Janet W. Zuber (Amana, Iowa: Amana Church Society, 1976), pp. 8–83.

16. The relation of pietism to the Enlightenment has been the subject of some debate. Some see the two apparently disparate intellectual forces not as direct opponents but rather as challengers of the dominant church orthodoxy, the first in some form preparing the way for the second. See Dominique Bourel, "Orthodoxie, Pietisme, Aufklärung," *Dix-huitième Siècle* 10 (1978): 27–32.

17. Pietism must bear part of the blame for its decline by its becoming overly rigid. Sagarra notes that in her comic satire "Pietism in a Whalebone Coat" Frau Gottschied introduces such comic characters of pietist devotion as Frau Glaubeleichtin (Mrs. Believe-anything), Frau Seufzerin (Mrs. Sigh), and Frau Zankenheimin (Mrs. Quarrel-home), all under the spell of the rapacious preacher Herr Scheinfromm (Mr. Seempious). Sagarra, *Social History of Germany*, p. 115.

18. Theodore Hamerow, *Restoration, Revolution, Reaction: Economics and Politics in Germany, 1815–1871* (Princeton: Princeton University Press, 1958). Hamerow rightly reminds us that agrarian terms and conditions varied greatly by region and province. The conditions discussed here were found largely in the West and the South, including the states of Baden, Württemberg, and Hesse-Darmstadt.

19. While the peasants' social status, economic chances, and legal position were all undergoing these major changes, the image of the peasant experienced a similar transformation, moving from that of outcast to a sort of folk hero incorporated within a larger rural ideology. See Gagliardo, *From Pariah to Patriot*.

20. Eda Sagarra, *A Social History of Germany, 1648–1840* (New York: Holmes and Meier, 1977), p. 142.

21. Peter Burke also sees the guilds as providing a common culture of values, symbols, and ceremonies that were progressively destroyed as the new economic order undermined their authority and coherence (*Popular Culture in Early Modern Europe*). Eda Sagarra believes that by 1815 the guilds had already lost most of their legal and economic power, though they might still have served a social function in giving their members a sense of corporate solidarity. But even this social benefit was being lost as the guilds degenerated into a purely restrictive role. Again, such trends varied by craft and by region. Sagarra, *Social History of Germany* (Brit. ed.), pp. 328–29.

22. Hamerow, *Restoration, Revolution, Reaction*, p. 21.

23. One must hesitate to generalize about the structure of peasant communities. As Jerome Blum has written, "Their great number, the many differences among them, the obscurity which veils so much of the history of Europe's peasantry, are a sampling of the obstacles which con-

spire to make definitive conclusions about the village community diffi-
cult if not impossible." Blum, "The Internal Structure and Polity of the
Village Community from the Fifteenth to the Nineteenth Century,"
Journal of Modern History 43 (1971): 541. For a full description of these
practices, see also Jerome Blum, "The European Village as Community:
Origins and Functions," *Agricultural History* 45 (1971): 157–78.

24. Hamerow, *Restoration, Revolution, Reaction*, p. 30.

25. Curiously, at roughly the same time that political theorists and religious writers were praising the peasant's "natural" piety and virtue,
others, including members of the middle classes, were concerned about
what they saw as the decline in peasant morality. In a revealing article
Edward Shorter describes how these individuals traced the alarming
growth in population, especially among lower classes, to a rise in illegitimacy and a decline in morality in general. Illegitimacy does indeed
appear to have been on the increase, not because of what the middle
classes saw as the lower classes' "wantonness and laziness," but rather
because of the profound breakdown of traditional village structures, including changes in property and inheritance, new religious interpretations, and the beginnings of urbanization with the suggestion of pro-
letarization. For more on the crisis in morals see Edward Shorter,
"Middle Class Anxiety in the German Revolution of 1848," *Journal of
Social History* 2 (1969): 189–216, and J. Michael Phayer, "Lower Class
Morality: The Case of Bavaria," *Journal of Social History* 8 (1974):
79–95.

26. Hamerow, *Restoration, Revolution, Reaction*, p. 20.

27. Ibid.

28. Sagarra, *Social History of Germany* (Brit. ed.), p. 204.

29. John D. Post, *The Last Great Subsistence Crisis in the Western
World* (Baltimore: Johns Hopkins Press, 1977). For more on economic
developments throughout nineteenth-century Germany, see Helmut
Boehme, *An Introduction to the Social and Economic History of Ger-
many: Politics and Economic Change in the Nineteenth and Twentieth
Centuries*, trans. W. R. Lee (Oxford: Basil Blackwell, 1977).

30. These conditions helped trigger the first wave of nineteenth-
century emigration, particularly from the province of Swabia, where
whole villages would uproot and head for Russia or for the United States.
Of particular interest are the religious groups known as "Harmonies";
some of these were communal, and most set out for Russia to form their
pious communities. Curiously, other provinces, such as the Hesses, that
were experiencing the same objective economic distress did not suc-
cumb to this "emigration fever." See Mack Walker, *Germany and the*

Emigration, 1816–1865 (Cambridge: Harvard University Press, 1965), pp. 13–15.

31. Shambaugh, *Amana That Was and Amana That Is*, pp. 35–38.

32. Francis Alan Duval, "Christian Metz, German-American Religious Leader and Pioneer" (Ph.D. dissertation, University of Iowa, 1948), p. 54.

33. William Rufus Perkins and Barthinius L. Wick, *History of the Amana Society*, first published 1891 (New York: Arno Press, 1975), p. 35.

34. Ibid., p. 36.

35. Andelson, "Communalism and Change," pp. 31–37.

36. Pietism appealed to women because it gave them independent religious identity and an active role at a time when some theologians were still debating whether women had souls. As Sagarra writes, "Not only did Pietist preachers bring women to the conventicles, but they had them speak there about their religious experiences; the stress on feeling rather than understanding as a vehicle of experience appealed to many women, as did the intimate contact between souls." Sagarra, *Social History of Germany* (Brit. ed.), pp. 408–9.

37. Perkins and Wick, *History of the Amana Society*, p. 39.

38. Ibid., p. 40.

39. Duval, "Christian Metz," p. 106.

40. Translation supplied by the Amana Church Society.

41. Andelson, "Communalism and Change," p. 89.

42. Charles Nordhoff, *Communistic Societies of the United States*, first published 1875 (London: Hilary House, 1960), p. 28.

43. Andelson, "Communalism and Change," p. 91.

44. Shambaugh, *Amana That Was and Amana That Is*, p. 337.

45. Ibid., p. 58.

46. Duval, "Christian Metz," pp. 82–83.

47. The Inspirationists fit Walker's description of emigrants as neither the best off nor the worst. Besides many recruits from among the artisans and lower ranks, they had also attracted several well-to-do merchants and weavers. Sagarra provides a description of the life of early entrepreneurs, who in this period were often much attracted to the pietist revival (1820s–1830s). She describes such entrepreneurs as "patriarchal in character, simple, even frugal in everyday-life" and as dominating not just the economic life but also the religious life of their communities. See Sagarra, *Social History of Germany* (Brit. ed.), pp. 292–94.

48. Walker, *Germany and the Emigration*, p. 69. In some cases whole

villages that wanted to leave were bought out by their former feudal
lords, with, as Walker ironically remarks, "capitalist privilege and power
replacing feudal privilege and power" (p. 77).

49. Hamerow, *Restoration, Revolution, Reaction*, pp. 34–35.

CHAPTER 2

1. For this brief survey of early-nineteenth-century communes I consulted a number of sources. See my Bibliographical Essay for suggested
readings.

2. Perkins and Wick, *History of the Amana Society*, p. 44.

3. Ahlstrom, *Religious History of the American People*, p. 498.

4. The Mormons were not, however, communal during this period of
their history. See Klaus J. Hansen, *Mormonism and the American Experience* (Chicago: University of Chicago Press, 1981).

5. The Second Great Awakening has been the subject of considerable
intellectual debate. One of the earliest histories, still considered a classic
text, is Whitney R. Cross's *The Burned-over District: A Social and Intellectual History of Enthusiastic Religion in Western New York, 1800–
1830* (Ithaca: Cornell University Press, 1950). See also Lois W. Banner,
"Religious Benevolence as Social Control: A Critique of an Interpretation," *Journal of American History* 55 (June 1973): 23–41; Donald G.
Matthrews, "The Second Great Awakening as an Organizing Process,
1780–1830," *American Quarterly* 21 (Spring 1969): 23–43; and
Paul E. Johnson, *A Shopkeeper's Millennium: Society and Revivals in
Rochester, New York, 1815–1837* (New York: Hill and Wang, 1978).

6. David M. Ellis, James A. Frost, Harold G. Syrett, and Harry J. Car-
man, *A Short History of New York State* (Ithaca: Cornell University
Press, 1957), p. 281.

7. Frank J. Lankes, *The Ebenezer Society* (West Seneca, N.Y.: West
Seneca Historical Society, 1963), pp. 6–16.

8. Ibid., p. 16.

9. Ibid., p. 18.

10. Ibid., pp. 39–43.

11. Andelson, "Communalism and Change," p. 42.

12. Ibid., pp. 43–48.

13. Lankes, *Ebenezer Society*, p. 22.

14. Duval, cited in Andelson, "Communalism and Change," p. 50.

15. Shambaugh, *Amana That Was and Amana That Is*, pp. 66–67.

16. Andelson, "Communalism and Change," p. 51.

17. Rosabeth Moss Kanter, *Commitment and Community: Communes and Utopias in Sociological Perspective* (Cambridge: Harvard University Press, 1972).

18. Andelson, "Communalism and Change," pp. 129–49, passim.

19. Ibid., pp. 267–76.

20. Rosabeth Moss Kanter, ed., *Communes* (New York: Harper and Row, 1973).

21. Andelson, "Communalism and Change," p. 47.

22. For a contrasting view of the communal organization of "women's work," see Lionel Tiger and Joseph Shepher, *Women in the Kibbutz* (New York: Harcourt Brace Jovanovich, 1975).

23. Lankes, *Ebenezer Society*, p. 110. Lankes describes Mayer, a former member of Zoar who had grown dissatisfied with that community and gained acceptance into the Ebenezer society, as an "able businessman" with good English skills and an understanding of the legal system.

24. H. Perry Smith, *History of the City of Buffalo and Erie County*, vol. 1 (Syracuse, N.Y.: D. Mason, 1884), p. 229.

25. Ibid., p. 506.

26. Ibid.

27. Henry Wayland Hill, ed., *Municipality of Buffalo, New York: A History, 1720–1923*, vol. 1 (New York: Lewis Historical Publishing Company, 1923), p. 295.

28. See Stuart M. Blumin, *The Urban Threshold* (Chicago: University of Chicago Press, 1976).

29. Andelson, "Communalism and Change," p. 58.

30. Ibid.

31. Ellis et al., *Short History of New York State*, pp. 284–86.

32. Andelson, "Communalism and Change," p. 57.

33. Smith, *History of Buffalo*, pp. 505–7. Lankes also suggests that there were plans for a railroad to be built cutting through Ebenezer land. Lankes, *Ebenezer Society*.

CHAPTER 3

1. Morton M. Rosenberg, *Iowa on the Eve of the Civil War: A Decade of Frontier Politics* (Norman: University of Oklahoma Press, 1972), p. 28.

2. There is considerable debate about the extent of antislavery sentiment among the German population and its source. See Thomas J. Kelson, "The German-American Vote in the Election of 1860: The Case of

Indiana with Supporting Data from Ohio" (Ph.D. dissertation, Ball State University, 1967); Joel H. Silbey, "Pro-Slavery Sentiment in Iowa, 1838–1861" (master's thesis, State University of Iowa, 1956); George H. Daniels, "The Immigrant Vote in the 1860 Election: The Case of Iowa," *Mid-America* 44 (1962): 146–62; and Charles W. Emergy, "The Iowa Germans in the Election of 1860," *Annals of Iowa*, 3d ser., 22 (1940): 421–53. Rosenberg suggests that while German-American leaders may have encouraged a move to the Republican party, many German voters actually maintained their allegiance to the Democratic party, in part in reaction against the nativism associated with the Republicans, in part because of the "specter of racial competition." Rosenberg, *Iowa on the Eve of the Civil War*, p. 236.

3. Rosenberg, *Iowa on the Eve of the Civil War*, p. 6.

4. Ibid., pp. 10–12.

5. Hildegard Binder Johnson, "The Location of German Immigrants in the Middle West," *Annals of the Association of American Geographers* 41 (March 1951): 1–41.

6. Ibid., p. 40.

7. Shambaugh, *Amana That Was and Amana That Is*, pp. 72–77.

8. Arthur Bestor argues that it was not the frontier per se but rather the idea of the frontier that gave rise to communitarian experiments. Recruits to communitarian groups in both settled and frontier areas shared certain assumptions and outlooks, most significantly that social institutions were malleable and that one of the best ways of changing the social order for the better was by small working example communities, what Bestor terms "patent-office models of the good society." It is worth noting, however, that he grants that "the handful of communities that were actually located in or near the frontier zones were all planted there by groups from farther east or from Europe," and that for such groups that frontier operated as "a passive force—an area of relatively cheap land or relatively few restrictions." See Arthur E. Bestor, Jr., "Patent-Office Models of the Good Society: Some Relationships between Social Reform and Westward Expansion," *American Historical Review* 58 (April 1953): 505–26.

9. The settlement at Kalona would throughout its history be confused with the Amana Colonies. Tourists to Amana today are often disappointed to see the "natives" in everyday street dress as opposed to Amish costume and often also remark on the absence of horse-drawn buggies. For the most thorough study of the Iowa Amish, see Elmer and Dorothy Schwieder, *A Peculiar People: Iowa's Old Order Amish* (Ames: Iowa State University Press, 1975).

10. Martha Browning Smith, "The Story of Icaria," in *Patterns and Perspectives in Iowa History*, ed. Dorothy Schwieder, pp. 231–62 (Ames: Iowa State University Press, 1973).

11. Two of the most interesting works on land speculation in Iowa are Robert P. Swierenga, *Pioneers and Profits: Land Speculation on the Iowa Frontier* (Ames: Iowa State University Press, 1968), and Allan G. Bogue, *From Prairie to Corn Belt: Farming on the Illinois and Iowa Prairies in the Nineteenth Century* (Chicago: University of Chicago Press, 1963).

12. Milo Milton Quaife, ed., *The Early Days of Rock Island and Davenport: The Narratives of J. W. Spencer and J. M. D. Burrows* (Chicago: Lakeside Press, 1942).

13. Harly Ransom, ed., *Pioneer Recollections* (Cedar Rapids, Iowa: Historical Publishing Company, 1941), p. 41.

14. Ibid., p. 89.

15. For an excellent survey of the changing interpretation and significance of community in American life, see Thomas Bender, *Community and Social Change in America* (New Brunswick, N.J.: Rutgers University Press, 1978). See also other references in my Bibliographical Essay.

16. Union Historical Publishing Company, *A History of Iowa County* (Des Moines: Union Historical Publishing Company, 1881), p. 510.

17. Ibid.

18. T. Scott Miyakawa, *Protestants and Pioneers: Individualism and Conformity on the American Frontier* (Chicago: University of Chicago Press, 1964).

19. Union Historical Publishing Company, *History of Iowa County*, p. 102.

20. Ibid., p. 104.

21. Nordhoff, *Communistic Societies*, p. 32.

22. This item was in a family scrapbook, and I have been unable to trace the date.

23. Robert S. Fogarty, "American Communes, 1865–1914," *Journal of American Studies* 9 (1975): 145–62.

24. Ibid., p. 162.

CHAPTER 4

1. Kanter, *Commitment and Community*.

2. Andelson, "Communalism and Change," p. 107.

3. Shambaugh, *Amana That Was and Amana That Is*, pp. 209–12.

4. Ibid., pp. 199–208.

5. Perkins and Wick, *History of the Amana Society*, p. 74.

6. A delightful short account of the James brothers' stopover at South Amana is to be found in Harly Ransom's *Pioneer Recollections* (Cedar Rapids, Iowa: Historical Publishing Company, 1941), p. 96.

7. Ransom, *Pioneer Recollections*, p. 136.

8. Andelson, "Communalism and Change," p. 451.

9. Shambaugh, *Amana That Was and Amana That Is*, p. 135.

10. Nordhoff, *Communistic Societies*, p. 36.

11. The sexual patterns of communal societies have attracted considerable attention, in part because of their divergence from the norms of the outside society, in part because they reflect the underlying tension between "special affection" among specific members and attachment to community members at large. See, for example, Lawrence Foster, *Religion and Sexuality: Three American Communal Experiments of the Nineteenth Century* (New York: Oxford University Press, 1980), Lewis Coser, *Greedy Institutions* (New York: Free Press, 1974), and Kanter, *Commitment and Community*. See also Maren Lockwood Carden, *Oneida: Utopian Community to Modern Corporation* (New York: Harper and Row, 1971), and Flo Morse, *The Shakers and the World's People* (New York: Dodd, Mead, 1980).

12. Letter on file at the Museum of Amana Heritage.

13. See Carden, *Oneida*.

14. Andelson, "Communalism and Change," p. 183.

15. Ibid., p. 311.

16. Ibid., p. 315.

17. Shambaugh, *Amana That Was and Amana That Is*, pp. 288–93.

18. Nordhoff, *Communistic Societies*, p. 41.

19. Various methods have been used to test the mettle of new communal members. See the description of admission procedures among the Bruderhof in Benjamin Zablocki's *The Joyful Community* (Baltimore: Penguin, 1971).

20. As elsewhere in the text, the names of members and former members have been changed.

21. Andelson, "Communalism and Change," p. 84. See also Ruth Shonle Cavan, "Roles of the Old in Personal and Impersonal Societies," *Family Coordinator* 27 (1978): 315–19.

22. As Kanter demonstrates, such oral histories serve as powerful mechanisms to help transmit the dedication of the founding members to younger generations (*Commitment and Community*). For an understanding of how this process works on the Israeli kibbutz, see Amia Lieblich, *Kibbutz Makom* (New York: Pantheon, 1981).

23. Ronald Blythe, *The View in Winter* (New York: Harcourt Brace Jovanovich, 1979).

CHAPTER 5

1. Letter on exhibit in the Museum of Amana History.
2. Samuel Hays, *The Response to Industrialism, 1885–1914* (Chicago: University of Chicago Press, 1957), p. 1.
3. Ibid., p. 2.
4. Robert H. Wiebe, *The Search for Order: 1877–1920* (New York: Hill and Wang, 1967), p. xiii. Wiebe's concept of "island communities" and vision of a nineteenth-century America characterized by stability and order have been challenged by Stephen Thernstrom and Peter Knight, who emphasize instead the considerable population mobility of the period. In a case study of one Illinois town, Richard Alcorn resolves the apparent contradiction and in the process provides an intriguing look at sources of leadership, political power, and social order. See Richard S. Alcorn, "Leadership and Stability in Mid-Nineteenth Century America: A Case Study of an Illinois Town," *Journal of American History* 61 (1974–75): 685–702.
5. Wiebe, *Search for Order*, p. xiii.
6. Hays, *Response to Industrialism*, p. 15.
7. Myrtle Beinhauer, "Development of the Grange in Iowa, 1868–1930," in *Patterns and Perspectives in Iowa History*, ed. Dorothy Schwieder, pp. 207–30.
8. Sage, *History of Iowa*, p. 214.
9. Ibid., pp. 201–2, 217–18.
10. Ibid., p. 218.
11. Sage, *History of Iowa*, p. 254.
12. William E. Leuchtenberg, *The Perils of Prosperity, 1914–1932* (Chicago: University of Chicago Press, 1958).
13. Ibid., p. 101.
14. Cf. David Flint, *The Hutterites: A Study in Prejudice* (Toronto: Oxford University Press, 1975); John A. Hostetler, *Hutterite Society* (Baltimore: Johns Hopkins University Press, 1974); and John W. Bennett, *Hutterian Brethren: The Agricultural Economy and Social Organization of a Communal People* (Stanford: Stanford University Press, 1967).
15. Andelson, "Communalism and Change," pp. 357–60.
16. Ibid., p. 356.
17. Ibid., p. 360.

18. Ibid.

19. Ibid., p. 362.

20. Ibid., p. 363.

21. Disasters figured in the downfall or serious undermining of many communal efforts. Brook Farm and Northampton communes dissolved after major fires, though Harmony and several Shaker settlements managed to survive disasters including both floods and fire. Major diseases such as malaria and cholera could also pose serious threats, as they did to Bethel, several Shaker settlements, and Zoar. See Kanter, *Commitment and Community*, pp. 139–42.

22. Andelson, "Communalism and Change," p. 336.

CHAPTER 6

1. For a good introduction to the complex debate on secularization, see David Martin, *A General Theory of Secularization* (New York: Harper and Row, 1978).

2. Richard Hofstadter, *Anti-intellectualism in American Life* (New York: Vintage Books, 1963), p. 268.

3. Robert Peel, *Christian Science: Its Encounters with American Culture* (New York: Holt, Rinehart and Winston, 1966).

4. Letter in private ownership.

5. *Inspirations-Historie*, vol. 7 (1916), p. 119.

6. Flo Morse, *The Shakers and the World's People* (New York: Dodd, Mead, 1980), pp. 260–62.

7. Andelson, "Communalism and Change," p. 346.

8. Ibid., p. 347.

9. Ibid.

10. Ibid., p. 352.

11. Ibid.

CHAPTER 7

1. For an introduction to the historical thinking on modernization, see Kenneth A. Lockridge, "The American Revolution, Modernization, and Man: A Critique," in *Tradition, Conflict, and Modernization: Perspectives on the American Revolution*, ed. Richard Maxwell Brown and Don E. Fehrenbacher (New York: Academic Press, 1977). See also Seymour Martin Lipset, *The First New Nation* (New York: W. W. Norton,

1979), and Cyril E. Black, *The Dynamics of Modernization* (New York: Harper and Row, 1967).

2. George Mills, *Rogues and Heroes from Iowa's Amazing Past* (Ames: Iowa State University Press, 1977), p. 173.

3. Michael Berger, *The Devil Wagon in God's Country: The Automobile and Social Change in Rural America 1893–1929* (Hamden, Conn.: Shoestring Press, 1979).

4. See Warren James Belasco, *Americans on the Road: From Autocamp to Motel, 1910–1945* (Cambridge: MIT Press, 1979).

5. Mills, *Rogues and Heroes*, pp. 19–20. For more on Carrie Chapman Catt's Iowa background, see Louise Noun, "1872–1920—Carrie Chapman Catt," in *Patterns and Perspectives*, ed. Dorothy Schwieder.

6. See Carl Degler, *At Odds* (New York: Oxford University Press, 1981).

7. Theodore Dreiser, *Sister Carrie*, ed. Donald Pizer (New York: W. W. Norton, 1970), p. 17.

8. Ernest Sackville Turner, *The Shocking History of Advertising!* (London: M. Joseph, 1952).

9. See Dolores Hayden, *The Grand Domestic Revolution: A History of Feminist Designs for American Homes, Neighborhoods, and Cities* (Cambridge: MIT Press, 1981).

10. See Elizabeth H. Pleck and Joseph H. Pleck, *The American Man* Englewood Cliffs, N.J.: Prentice-Hall, 1980).

11. Clarence A. Andrews, "Did You Ever See a Dream Walking?" in *Growing up in Iowa: Reminiscences of Fourteen Iowa Authors*, ed. Clarence A. Andrews (Ames: Iowa State University Press, 1978), p. 101.

12. Mills, *Rogues and Heroes*, pp. 185–86.

13. Winifred D. Wandersee, *Women's Work and Family Values, 1920–1940* (Cambridge: Harvard University Press, 1981).

14. Robert and Helen Lynd, *Middletown: A Study in American Culture* (New York: Harcourt, Brace, 1929), pp. 251–314.

15. Union Historical Company, *History of Iowa County*, p. 510.

16. Andelson, "Communalism and Change," p. 323.

17. Barbara Yambura, *A Change and a Parting* (Ames: Iowa State University Press, 1960), pp. 264–65.

CHAPTER 8

1. For two intriguing and contrasting looks at the contemporary status of the American dream, see James Oliver Robertson, *American Myth,*

American Reality (New York: Hill and Wang, 1980), and also Studs Terkel, *American Dreams: Lost and Found* (New York: Pantheon, 1980).

2. Hostetler, *Hutterite Society*, pp. 273–75; John A. Hostetler, *Amish Society*, 3d. ed. rev. (Baltimore: Johns Hopkins University Press, 1980), pp. 292–312.

CHAPTER 9

1. Lawrence Rettig, *Amana Today* (Amana, Iowa: Amana Society, 1975). Rettig does not provide any clues about why the vote in Middle Amana differs so radically from those taken in the other villages. Some residents suggested the elders in Middle were more opposed to the change; others, that Middle residents, living as they did toward the center of the colonies, were more conservative than those in colonies like Homestead or West Amana that were more exposed to the outside world.

2. Rettig, *Amana Today*, p. 123.

3. Ibid., p. 18.

4. Ibid., pp. 42–47.

5. Maren Lockwood Carden, *Oneida: Utopian Community to Modern Corporation* (New York: Harper and Row, 1971), pp. 89–111.

6. Ibid., pp. 124–32.

7. Rettig, *Amana Today*, p. 21.

8. See Arthur Barlow's pamphlet "The Amana Society's 'Great Change'," 1971.

9. Rettig, *Amana Today*, pp. 43–44.

CHAPTER 10

1. Richard Hofstadter, *The Age of Reform* (New York: Random House, 1955), p. 24.

2. Henry Nash Smith, *Virgin Land: The American West as Symbol and Myth* (New York: Random House, 1950), p. 219.

3. Charles R. Hearn, *The American Dream in the Great Depression* (Westport, Conn.: Greenwood Press, 1977).

4. See Arthur Schlesinger, *The Crisis of the Old Order* (New York: Houghton Mifflin, 1957), and William Manchester, *The Glory and the Dream* (Boston: Little, Brown, 1974).

5. The newspaper articles quoted are from a collection available at the Museum of Amana History.

6. John L. Shover, "The Communist Party and the Midwest Farm Crisis of 1933," *Journal of American History* 51 (1964–65): 248–66.

7. Smith, *Virgin Land*, p. 139.

8. Hofstadter, *Age of Reform*, p. 40.

9. Peter Stuck, "Amana Protests" (letter to the editor), *Christian Century* 52 (1935): 1212.

10. Ibid.

11. Nelson Antrim Crawford, "Communism Goes Broke in Iowa," *American Magazine* 142 (1946): 44–45.

12. Ibid., p. 107.

13. Martin Dickel, "Communal Life in Amana," *Iowa Journal of History* 59 (1961): 83–89.

CHAPTER 11

1. Rettig, *Amana Today*, pp. 42–47.

2. See Edward Shils, *Center and Periphery: Essays in Macrosociology* (Chicago: University of Chicago Press, 1975).

3. Social dancing was also controversial outside the Amanas, and roadside dance halls were seen as places of sin where strangers might tempt local sons and daughters. See Michael Berger, *The Devil Wagon in God's Country: The Automobile and Social Change in Rural America, 1893–1929* (Hamden, Conn.: Shoestring Press, 1979).

4. Rettig, *Amana Today*, p. 27.

5. The Rural Electrification Act was one of the few 1930s social programs from which Iowa benefited in proportion to its population compared with other states, and extensive electrification occurred throughout the 1930s.

6. On 23 May 1918 the governor of Iowa had passed an edict forbidding the use of foreign languages, even in private conversations—an edict aimed largely at Iowa's German population. See Sage, *History of Iowa*, p. 252.

7. Iowa's response to World War II was in general one of enthusiastic support. See Sage, *History of Iowa*.

CHAPTER 12

1. For a good introduction to this difficult transition, see David Martin, *A General Theory of Secularization* (New York: Harper and Row, 1978).

2. Rettig, *Amana Today*, pp. 62–63.

3. Ibid., p. 54.

4. Ibid., pp. 55–56.

5. See Hostetler, *Hutterite Society*.

6. Besides Heinemann-Landmann, there were three other female *Werkzeuge*, all during the unstable years 1714–17. The inspiration of the first two lasted approximately four months each; the inspiration of the third lasted approximately four and a half years. See Francis Alan Duval, "Christian Metz, German-American Religious Leader and Pioneer" (Ph.D. dissertation, State University of Iowa, 1948).

7. See Victor Turner, *The Ritual Process* (Chicago: Aldine, 1969), for some interesting thoughts on why this should be so.

8. Rettig, *Amana Today*, p. 61.

9. This desire to restrict English relates to Kanter's point regarding the use of mystery to increase the feeling of transcendence and, through it, commitment. See Kanter, *Commitment and Community*.

10. Women are often encouraged to maintain distinctive ethnic dress, to serve as folklore, long after men have abandoned this dress and this role and adopted modern attire and behaviors. See, for example, Valene L. Smith, ed., *Hosts and Guests: The Anthropology of Tourism* (Philadelphia: University of Pennsylvania Press, 1977).

11. Rettig, *Amana Today*, p. 61.

12. See Theodore Caplow, Howard M. Bahr, and Bruce A. Chadwick, "Piety in Middletown," *Society* 130 (January–February 1981): 34–37, for a somewhat contrasting view of contemporary religiosity.

13. Donald G. Bloesch, *The Evangelical Renaissance* (Grand Rapids, Mich.: William B. Eerdmans, 1973).

14. Conor Cruise O'Brien, "Mystique and Politics," *New York Times*, 22 August 1979, p. A23.

CHAPTER 13

1. Rettig, *Amana Today*, pp. 18–21.

2. Ibid., pp. 42–43.

3. Ibid., pp. 44–46.

4. Ibid.

5. Ibid., pp. 110–11.

6. The account that follows is culled from newspaper articles on file at the Museum of Amana History and from interviews both with involved parties and with other residents.

7. This is certainly not to suggest any teleological explanation of Amana's survival as a community. As in Oneida, given the choices that had already been made, the remaining choices available to the community residents were narrowed, and the corporation option in these circumstances was particularly appealing.

CHAPTER 14

1. Dean MacCannell, *The Tourist* (New York: Schocken Books, 1976).

2. Ronald Blythe, *The View in Winter* (New York: Harcourt Brace Jovanovich, 1979).

3. Rettig, *Amana Today*, p. 109. See also Warren Belasco, *Americans on the Road: From Autocamp to Motel, 1910–1945* (Cambridge: MIT Press, 1979).

4. For some of the material that follows I consulted documents on file with the Amana Travel Council.

5. Flo Morse, *The Shakers and the World's People* (New York: Dodd, Mead, 1980), pp. 283–86.

CHAPTER 15

1. Dolores Hayden, *Seven American Utopias: The Architecture of Communitarian Societies, 1790–1975* (Cambridge: MIT Press, 1976), p. 254.

2. Much of the information that follows was gathered from records of the Amana Heritage Society and the Landmark Committee, from the printed Master Plan for the Amana Colonies, and from interviews conducted during the summers of 1977–79.

3. According to one committee member, the firm was selected because "of the three finalists, we felt they were probably more in a position to work directly with us rather than send in someone else and have administrative costs. They were very personable; the graphics were outstanding too. They were our unanimous choice on the basis of their experience as well as these other factors."

4. Preservation in other rural areas also bears the mark of rugged individualism. See Jane Silverman, "Rural America—Love It or Lose It," *Historic Preservation* 33 (March–April 1981): 24–31.

5. See Diane L. Barthel, "The Role of Ethnicity," in *Social Standing in America*, ed. Lee Rainwater and Richard P. Coleman, pp. 92–116 (New York: Basic Books, 1978).

6. See Carolyn Ellis, "Community, Crabs, and Capitalism" (Ph.D. dissertation, State University of New York at Stony Brook, 1981).

CONCLUSION

1. Perkins and Wick, *History of the Amana Society*, p. 64.
2. Ibid., p. 65.
3. Ibid., p. 67.
4. *Moline Daily Dispatch*, 23 December 1936. See also chapter 10.
5. Richard D. Lyons, Conservative Sects Find Homes in New York," *New York Times*, 3 October 1981, p. 29, cols. 1–4.
6. Roland Barthes, *Mythologies* (New York: Hill and Wang, 1972), p. 159.
7. Paul Ricoeur, quoted in Richard H. Brown, *A Poetic for Sociology* (Cambridge: Cambridge University Press, 1977), p. 48.

Bibliographical Essay

Much of my research on Amana was based on oral histories, focused interviews, and documents on file with Amana organizations such as the Landmark Committee and the Travel Council. In addition I made use of documents at the Museum of Amana History, including the yearly *Inspirations-Histories*, the post-Change Amana Society *Bulletins*, miscellaneous letters, and newspaper articles from the periods of the Change and the 1978 lawsuit. Janet Zuber's translation of the early volumes of the *Inspirations-Histories* was most useful as I assessed the dynamics of the early period and the early-nineteenth-century revival. I also relied on the nearby Marengo Public Library for early twentieth-century newspapers and descriptions of Iowa County pioneer life.

Extensive analysis of Amana church documents and documents relating to the economic structure and problems of the old Amana had been already carried out by Jonathan Gary Andelson in his excellent Ph.D. dissertation "Communalism and Change in the Amana Society, 1855–1932" (University of Michigan, 1974). I am much indebted to him for his careful analysis of Amana social structure and of internal developments leading up to the Change. More readily accessible is Bertha Shambaugh's favorable treatment, *Amana That Was and Amana That Is*. The first part was written in 1908 and later was combined with a post-Change evaluation of the society in 1932 (Iowa City: State Historical Society of Iowa). Amana also figures among the communal societies described by Charles Nordhoff in his now-classic *The Communistic Societies of the United States*, first published in 1875 (New York: Schocken, 1965), and also in William Alfred Hinds's *American Communities*, first published in 1878 (Secaucus, N.J.: Citadel Press, 1961). Somewhat less readily accessible but particularly interesting for its reflection of late-nineteenth-century attitudes toward the community is *History of the Amana Society*, by William Rufus Perkins and Barthinius L. Wick, originally published in 1891 and reprinted in 1975 by the Arno Press (New York). Two insiders have written about Amana life and social structure: Barbara Yambura in her fictionalized account of pre-Change life, *A Change and a Parting* (Ames: Iowa State University Press, 1960), and Lawrence Rettig in his description of post-Change Amana, *Amana Today*, published by the Amana Society in 1975. Wallace Christen's little-known and often negative consideration, *Inspirationist Mysticism: The Amana Community* (Lockport, Ill.: Ogren Press, 1975) serves as a counterpoint to Shambaugh, but Andelson's dissertation provides the most scholarly and balanced treatment of life in the colonies. Francis Alan Duval's dissertation, "Christian Metz, German-American Religious Leader and Pioneer" (University of Iowa, 1948), is a largely favorable treatment of the community's leader. Also see Frank J. Lankes, *The Ebenezer Society* (West Seneca, N.Y.: West Seneca Historical Society, 1963), for discussion of the Inspirationist purchase and settlement of the New York tract, Arthur Barlow's pamphlet describing his role in the Great Change ("The Amana Society's 'Great Change'," published privately, 1971), and Tom and Mary Phillips, *Amana, Metamorphosis of a Culture* (Cedar Rapids, Iowa: Kirkwood Community College, 1973). In addition, a number of shorter treatments of Amana history have appeared in Iowa publications and journals. See, for example, Richard Ely, "Study of Religious Communalism," *Palimpsest* 52 (1971): 177–97; Martin Dickel, "Communal Life in Amana," *Iowa Journal of History* (1961): 3–89; and William Petersen, "Life in the Amana Colony," *Palimpsest* 52 (1971): 161–224.

Amana art and architecture have attracted specialist attention. Particularly noteworthy and enlightening is Dolores Hayden's chapter on Amana in her *Seven American Utopias: The Architecture of Communitarian Societies, 1790–1975* (Cambridge: MIT Press, 1976). Interested readers might also consult Ruth Geraldine Snyder's master's thesis, "The Arts and Crafts of the Amana Society" (State University of Iowa, 1949), and Delmar Nordquist's master's thesis, "The Development of an Immigrant Community in Architecture, Arts and Crafts" (State University of Iowa, 1947). Linguists should note Lawrence Rettig's dissertation, "Grammatical Structures in Amana German" (University of Iowa, 1970), and Irving Rydell Johnson's dissertation, "A Study of the Amana Dialect" (University of Iowa, 1935). On other specialized topics one might consult Robert Edwin Clark's dissertation, "A Cultural and Historical Geography of the Amana Colonies" (University of Nebraska,

1974), and Irene C. Linder's master's thesis, "A Study of the Birth Rate of Amana" (University of Iowa, 1941).

Finally, social scientists have applied their theories to several aspects of Amana society. One of the earliest articles that attempted to outline the various ways Amana might serve as a useful case study was Grace S. Chaffee's "The Isolated Religious Sect as an Outlet for Social Research," *American Journal of Sociology* 35 (1930): 618–30. Gordon F. Streib and Ruth B. Streib consider the advantages Amana's elderly members enjoy in their article "Communes and the Aging: Utopian Dreams and Gerontological Reality," *American Behavioral Scientist* 19 (1975): 176–89, as does Ruth Shonle Cavan in her article "Roles of the Old in Personal and Impersonal Societies," *Family Coordinator* 27 (1978): 35–319. Shonle Cavan also describes some of the choices now facing the Amanas in her article "The Future of a Historic Commune: Amana," *International Review of Modern Sociology* 8 (1978): 89–101. Especially worth noting are two recent journal articles by Jonathan G. Andelson. In "The Double Bind and Social Change in Communal Amana," *Human Relations* 34 (1981): 111–25, he develops the central theme of his dissertation, while in "Routinization of Behavior in a Charismatic Leader," *American Ethnologist* 7 (1980): 716–33, he discusses the differing personal characteristics of Metz and Heinemann and the variation in their demonstration of inspiration by occasion and by village, differences that encouraged the greater veneration of Metz as a charismatic leader. Finally, Amana is cited an important example of a long-lived, successful commune by Rosabeth Moss Kanter in her theoretical work comparing the structures or "commitment mechanisms" developed by nineteenth- and twentieth-century communes, *Commitment and Community: Communes and Utopias in Sociological Perspective* (Cambridge: Harvard University Press, 1972).

While all these sources were useful and informative, I discovered that to understand the significance of Amana in terms of its history and its movement from the cultural boundary of American society to its integration as a symbol of progress and acceptance of national purpose, it was necessary to look outward from Amana toward the experience of other communal attempts and toward the larger processes of social change occurring throughout the society.

HISTORICAL BACKGROUND

Germany: I found that the most useful reference for understanding social conditions surrounding the foundation and early history of the Society of True Inspiration in the eighteenth and early nineteenth centuries was Eda Sagarra's *A Social History of Germany* (London: Methuen, 1977). Other general histories that proved valuable were Hajo Holborn's *A History of Modern Germany, 1648–1840* (London: Eyre and Spottiswoode, 1965), especially chapters 2, 6, 13, and 16; W. H. Bruford's *Germany in the Eighteenth Century: The Social Background of the Literary Revival* (Cambridge: Cambridge University Press, 1968); and Theodore Hamerow's *Restoration, Revolution, Reaction: Economics and Politics in Germany, 1815–1871* (Princeton: Princeton University Press, 1958). Regarding the economic conditions leading up to the period of emigration, see Helmut Boehme, *An Introduction to the Social and Economic History of Germany: Politics and Change in the Nineteenth and Twentieth Centuries* (Oxford: Basil Blackwell, 1978), especially chapters 1 and 2, and also John D. Post, *The Last Subsistence Crisis in the Western World* (Baltimore: Johns Hopkins Press, 1977). Somewhat less useful here but worth consulting are W. C. Conze's chapter "The Effects of Nineteenth Century Liberal Agrarian Reforms on Social Structure in Central Europe" and G. Adelmann's "Structural Changes in the Rhenish Linen and Cotton Trades at the Outset of Industrialization," both in *Essays in European Economic History* ed. F. Crouzet, W. H. Chaloner, and William Stern (New York: St. Martin's Press, 1970). For more detailed discussion of conditions giving rise to emigration see Mack Walker's *German Home Towns* (Ithaca: Cornell University Press, 1971) and also his *Germany and Emigration, 1816–1885* (Cambridge: Harvard University Press, 1964). For more specific references concerning the changing status of the peasants, the role of the guilds, village structure, and so forth, see my notes to chapter 1.

New York State: Much scholarship has been devoted to the religious enthusiasm surrounding the Second Great Awakening. Whitney R. Cross's *The Burned-over District* (Ithaca: Cornell University Press, 1950) is a still highly regarded history; Paul E. Johnson's *A Shopkeeper's Millennium* is a provocative examination of the relations among religious, political, and economic concerns (New York: Hill and Wang, 1978). Laurence Veysey's *The Perfectionists: Radical Social Thought in the North, 1815–1860*, taps a number of intellectual and religious currents (New York: John Wiley, 1973). I also consulted several local histories of the Buffalo area, including Henry Wayland Hill, ed., *Municipality of Buffalo, New York: A History, 1720–1923*, vol. 1 (New York: Lewis Historical Publishing Company, 1923); H. Perry Smith, ed., *History of the City of Buffalo and Erie County*, vol. 1 (Syracuse, N.Y.: D. Mason, 1884); and

Stephan Grehl, *Pioneers of Buffalo: Its Growth and Development* (Buffalo, N.Y.: Commission on Human Relations, 1966).

Iowa: For the broad outline of Iowa history I turned first to Leland Sage's *A History of Iowa* (Ames: Iowa State University Press, 1974), which deals mostly with political developments, and to the essays in Dorothy Schwieder, ed., *Patterns and Perspectives in Iowa History* (Ames: Iowa State University Press, 1973). Morton Rosenberg's *Iowa on the Eve of Civil War: A Decade of Frontier Politics* (Norman: University of Oklahoma Press, 1972) was useful in setting the stage for the Inspirationists' arrival, as was Hildegard Binder Johnson's article "The Location of German Immigrants in the Middle West," *Annals of the Association of American Geographers* 41 (1951): 1–41. Much good work has been done on Iowa land-use patterns. See especially Robert P. Swierenga's *Pioneers and Profits: Land Speculation on the Iowa Frontier* (Ames: Iowa State University Press, 1968); Donald Winters, "Tenant Farming in Iowa, 1860–1900: A Study of the Terms of Rental Leases," *Agricultural History* 48 (1974): 130–55; and Keach Johnson, "Iowa Dairying at the Turn of the Century: The New Agriculture and Progressivism," *Agricultural History* 45 (1971): 95–110. G. Riley has described the life of the Iowa frontierswoman in her articles "Images of the Frontierswoman: Iowa as a Case Study," *Western Historical Quarterly* 8 (1971): 189–202, and "Not Gainfully Employed: Women on the Iowa Frontier, 1833–1870," *Pacific Historical Review* 49 (1980): 237–64. In considering recent developments, along with Sage I recommend William Erbe, ed., *Urbanization, Migration, and Social Change: Iowa Enters the 1970's* (Iowa City: University of Iowa, 1973), and Harlan Hahn's *Urban-Rural Conflict* (Beverly Hills, Calif.: Sage Publications, 1971).

For more local background I consulted James C. Dinwiddie, *A History of Iowa County, Iowa, and Its People* (Chicago: S. J. Clarke, 1915), the Union Historical Company's *The History of Iowa County* (Des Moines, 1881), and the Iowa Board of Immigration's *Iowa: The Home for Immigrants* (Des Moines, 1870). Interesting glimpses of Iowa social life were provided by Harly Ransom's *Pioneer Recollections* (Cedar Rapids, Iowa: Historical Publishing Company, 1941) and by Milo Milton Quaife's editing of the recollections of J. W. Spencer and J. M. D. Burrows, *The Early Days of Rock Island and Davenport* (Chicago: Lakeside Press, 1942). For early-twentieth-century recollections see G. S. Mills, *Rogues and Heroes from Iowa's Amazing Past* (1977), Carl Hamilton, *In No Time at All* (1974), and Clarence Andrews, ed., *Growing Up in Iowa* (1978), all published at Ames by Iowa State University Press. I also recommend Ruth Suckow's *Iowa Interiors*, originally published in 1926, edited by Elizabeth Hardwick and reprinted by Arno Press in 1977 (New York).

Numerous other sources were useful in locating Amana history within the changing context of the midwestern community and small town. See especially Thomas Bender, *Community and Social Change in America* (New Brunswick, N.J.: Rutgers University Press, 1978), T. Scott Miyakawa, *Protestants and Pioneers: Individualism and Conformity on the American Frontier* (Chicago: University of Chicago Press, 1964), Herve Varenne, *Americans Together: Structural Diversity in a Midwestern Town* (New York: Teachers College Press, 1977), Richard Lingeman, *Small Town America* (New York: G. P. Putnam's Sons, 1980), and Noel Iverson, *Germania, USA: Social Change in New Ulm, Minnesota* (Minneapolis: University of Minnesota Press, 1966). I also recommend William Simon and John Gagnon's article "The Decline and Fall of the Small Town," *Trans-Action* 4 (1967): 42–51, and two sociological classics: Robert and Helen Lynd's *Middletown* (New York: Harcourt, Brace, 1929) and Arthur Vidich and Joseph Bensman's controversial *Small Town in Mass Society* (Princeton: Princeton University Press, 1968). Richard S. Alcorn's "Leadership and Stability in Mid-Nineteenth Century America," *Journal of American History* 61 (1974–75): 685–702, helped resolve the conflicting images of the nineteenth-century town as static and as extremely mobile. Warren Belasco's *Americans on the Road: From Autocamp to Motel, 1910–1945* (Cambridge: MIT Press, 1979) provided an entertaining history of the development of tourism and the role of the automobile. On the same subject one might also consult Michael Berger's *The Devil Wagon in God's Country: The Automobile and Social Change in Rural America, 1893–1929* (Hamden, Conn.: Shoestring Press, 1979) and Blaine A. Brownell's article, "A Symbol of Modernity: Attitudes toward the Automobile in Southern Cities in the 1920's," *American Quarterly* 24 (1972): 20–44.

OTHER COMMUNAL ATTEMPTS

Finally, for those in search of comparative material regarding other attempts at communal living, a wide range of studies are available. Some of the classic surveys include Charles Nordhoff's *The Communistic Societies of the United States*, first published 1875 (New York: Schocken, 1965), John Humphrey Noyes's *History of American Socialisms*, first published 1870 (New York: Dover Publications, 1966), William A.

Hinds's *American Communities*, first published 1878 (Secaucus, N.J.: Citadel Press), and Arthur Bestor's *Backwoods Utopias: The Sectarian Origins and the Owenite Phase of Communitarian Socialism in America, 1663–1829*, 2d ed. (Philadelphia: University of Pennsylvania Press, 1971). See also Mark Holloway's *Heaven on Earth: Utopian Communes in America, 1680–1880*, 2d ed. (New York: Dover Publications, 1966) and Lawrence Foster's recent comparative look at the Shakers, the Oneida Perfectionists, and the Mormons, *Religion and Sexuality in Three American Communal Experiments of the Late Nineteenth Century* (New York: Oxford University Press, 1981).

For material on some of the best-known nineteenth-century efforts, one might look to Edward D. Andrews, *The People Called the Shakers: A Search for the Perfect Society*, originally published by Oxford in 1953, reprinted by Dover Publications in 1963, and also Edward A. Andrews and Faith Andrews, *Work and Worship: The Economic Order of the Shakers* (Greenwich, Conn.: New York Graphic Society, 1974). William Sims Bainbridge uses census material to examine the changing demographic structure of the Shaker communities in his article "Shaker Demographics, 1840–1900: An Example of the Use of U.S. Census Enumeration Schedules," *Journal for the Scientific Study of Religion* 21 (December 1982): 352–65. Flo Morse's recent documentary history *The Shakers and the World's People* (New York: Dodd, Mead, 1980) is extremely interesting and informative, particularly regarding the reaction of the outside world to the Shaker settlements. For Oneida, see Maren Lockwood Carden's *Oneida: From Utopian Community to Modern Corporation* (New York: Harper and Row, 1971) and also Robert Fogarty, "Oneida: A Utopian Search for Religious Security," *Labor History* 14 (Spring 1973): 202–27, and Spencer Olin, "The Oneida Community and the Instability of Charismatic Authority," *Journal of American History* 67 (September 1980): 285–300. George B. Lockwood's *The New Harmony Movement*, first published 1905 (New York: Dover Publications, 1971), is a classic text on that communal society, and J. F. C. Harrison's *Robert Owen and the Owenites in Britain and America* puts the New Harmony experiment in proper comparative perspective. For other significant alternative societies one can turn to Karl Arndt's *George Rapp's Harmony Society, 1785–1847* (Philadelphia: University of Pennsylvania Press, 1965) and his later study, *George Rapp's Successors and Material Heirs, 1847–1916* (Cranbury, N.J.: Associated University Presses, 1971). See also Charles Le Warne's *Utopias on Puget Sound* (Seattle: University of Washington Press, 1975) and Richard Francis's article on Bronson Alcott's Fruitlands, "Circumstances and Salvation:

The Ideology of the Fruitlands Utopia," *American Quarterly* 25 (May 1973): 202–34. These are only some of the better-known communal efforts. Robert Fogarty's article "American Communes, 1865–1914," *Journal of American Studies* 9 (1975): 145–62, lists the total number and describes the variety of often lesser-known communes formed in the later nineteenth and early twentieth centuries. His *Dictionary of American Communal and Utopian History* (Westport, Conn.: Greenwood Press, 1980) is also a useful reference regarding communal leaders.

Under this general rubric, some of the most outstanding studies have dealt with the Mennonites and the Hutterites. John A. Hostetler's *Hutterite Society* (1974) and his *Amish Society*, both published at Baltimore by Johns Hopkins University Press, are particularly fine examples. One might also look to John Bennett's *Hutterian Brethren* (Stanford: Stanford University Press, 1967), and David Flint's examination of Hutterites in Canada, *The Hutterites: A Study in Prejudice* (Toronto: Oxford University Press, 1975). Regarding the Amish in Iowa, see Melvin Gingerich's *The Mennonites in Iowa* (Iowa City: State Historical Society, 1939) and Dorothy Schwieder and Elmer Schwieder's *A Peculiar People: Iowa's Old Order Amish* (Ames: Iowa State University Press, 1975). For the Iowa Icarians see Martha Browning Smith's chapter "The Story of Icaria" in *Patterns and Perspectives in Iowa History* ed. Dorothy Schwieder, pp. 231–61 (Ames: Iowa State University Press, 1973), and also Boris Blick and H. Roger Grant, "Life in New Icaria, Iowa," *Annals of Iowa* 42 (1974): 198–204.

Other studies of major religious communes lasting into the twentieth century include Benjamin Zablocki's look into the Bruderhof, *The Joyful Community* (Baltimore: Penguin, 1971), and Robert Fogarty's recent history *The Righteous Remnant: The House of David* (Kent, Ohio: Kent State University Press, 1981).

In addition, there is a substantial literature on the communes of the 1960s. One might start with Rosabeth Moss Kanter's *Commitment and Community* (Cambridge: Harvard University Press, 1972), in which she draws comparisons between nineteenth- and twentieth-century communes, then survey the range of articles in her edited volume *Communes* (New York: Harper and Row, 1973). Ruth Shonle Cavan and Man Singh Das have also edited a collection of articles dealing with communes in both major periods, *Communes: Historical and Contemporary* (New Delhi: Vikas Publishing House, 1979). Keith Melville's *Communes in the Counter Culture: Origins, Theories, Styles of Life* (New York: William Morrow, 1972) is highly accessible, and Bennett Berger's *Survival of a Counterculture* (Berkeley: University of California Press, 1981) provides an interesting counterpoint to the late 1960s enthusiasm. Finally, for an empirical analysis of 120 urban and rural communes, see Benjamin Zablocki, *Alienation and Charisma: A Study of Contemporary American Communes* (New York: Free Press, 1980).

Index